Birds of Vietnam

Wolfgang J. Daunicht

AVITOPIA, Prof. Dr. Wolfgang J. Daunicht
Max-Born-Straße 12, D-60438 Frankfurt am Main
Telefax: +49(69)90756638
E-Mail: admin@avitopia.de

Further information is available at

www.avitopia.net

Table of Contents

Preface

Vietnam is a souvereign State.

Vietnam is a predominantly mountainous, wooded country in the tropics of Southeast Asia. Fan-Si-Pan is the highest mountain of Vietnam and the Indo-Chinese peninsula with 3143 m. The geographical and climatic situation has produced a great avidiversity, and many species of birds have limited distribution areas. Therefore, BirdLife International has declared two areas of Vietnam Endemic Bird Areas (EBA). Besides, Vietnam has 30 national parks; the first and today one of the most important is Cuc Phuong in the alluvial plain of the Red River. There alone over 320 bird species have been recorded.

Vietnam contributes with several properties to the natural heritage of humanity. You can obtain informations about the importance of these properties on the following web pages of the UNESCO:

Ha Long Bay - https://whc.unesco.org/en/list/672

Phong Nha-Ke Bang National Park - https://whc.unesco.org/en/list/951

Trang An Landscape Complex - https://whc.unesco.org/en/list/1438

Vietnam has joined the UNESCO program to reconcile the conservation of biodiversity with its sustainable use. Biosphere reserves are being set up to promote this purpose. You can find information about these reserves on the following UNESCO website: https://en.unesco.org/biosphere/aspac#vietnam

If you want to assess the importance of individual areas of a country for bird life, the organization BirdLife International is particularly helpful. For this purpose, the terms IBA and EBA were coined. An IBA (Important Bird and Biodiversity Area) is an area of significant importance for the long-term conservation of global bird life. A list of the IBAs (Important Bird and Biodiversity Areas) of this country is available in the Data Zone of http://datazone.birdlife.org/site/results?cty=229. In this list you can call up a map and further information for each IBA with one click.An EBA (Endemic Bird Areas) is an area with two or more bird species with restricted distribution (<50 000km^2). A list of the EBAs extending to this country can be found at http://datazone.birdlife.org/eba/results?cty=229. Here informations about these EBAs and their particular bird species are offered.

Many wetlands around the world are protected under the Ramsar Convention to preserve habitat, particularly for waterfowl and shorebirds. A documentation of the country's Ramsar sites can be found on the website https://rsis.ramsar.org/sites/default/files/rsiswp_search/exports/Ramsar-Sites-annotated-summary-Viet-Nam.pdf. A map and short descriptions are offered here.

The assessment of the global conservation status of bird species uses the criteria of the Red List (IUCN) 2012.

Legend

△ Near threatened

▲ Vulnerable

▲ Endangered

▲ Critically endangered

▲ Extinct in the wild

▲ Data deficient

Ø Invalid taxon

† Extinct

ⓔ Picture of an endemic subspecies

🔊 Link to video with audio

☐ Link to video

🔊 Link to audio

This e-book is based on a request to the AVITOPIA Data Base the 22nd October 2023.

The request profile was:

 Primary language: English - Secondary language: unrestricted

 Maximum number of pictures per species: 1

 Content and illustration: all names, optimal illustration

 Scientific system: Clements et al. 2017

 Method of area selection: Menu tree

 Name of area: Vietnam

 Survival criterion: unrestricted

 Selection of a taxon: all birds

 Taxonomic depth: Species of Birds

 Selection of activity/nest/portrait: unrestricted

 Selection of plumage/egg(s): unrestricted

 Selection of image technique: unrestricted

In the resulting PDF or ePub file, resp., all index and register entries are linked.

Bird Topography

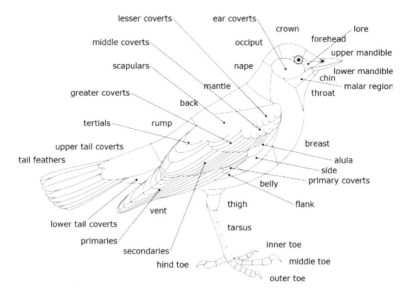

Species of Birds

Ducks and Geese - *Anatidae*

The family of Ducks and Geese occurs in all continents of the world except in Antarctica. The birds grow up to 30 - 180 cm long and live essentially on the water. The front three toes are webbed, the fourth toe is small and shifted upwards. All species swim, some dive well. Most species fly well, only a few are flightless. However, shortly after the breeding season, the birds adopt simple plumage and shed all flight feathers, so that they are unable to fly for some time. The nests are very diverse: there are nests on the ground, in ground caves, in steep walls and in tree hollows. The clutch comprises 4 to 12 eggs, the incubation lasts between 3 and 5 weeks and the young leave the nest soon after hatching.

Lesser Whistling Duck
  de:Javapfeifgans
  fr: Dendrocygne siffleur
  es:Suirirí de Java
  ja: リュウキュウガモ
  cn:栗树鸭
Dendrocygna javanica

♂♀ adult

Greylag Goose
  de:Graugans
  fr: Oie cendrée
  es: Ansar Común
  ja: ハイイロガン
  cn:灰雁
Anser anser

www.avitopia.net/bird.en/?vid=200305
www.avitopia.net/bird.en/?aud=200305

adult

Knob-billed Duck
  de:Glanzente
  fr: Canard à bosse
  es:Pato Crestudo
  ja: コブガモ
  cn:瘤鸭
Sarkidiornis melanotos

♂ adult

♀ adult

AU

Ruddy Shelduck
  de:Rostgans
  fr: Tadorne casarca
  es:Tarro Canelo
  ja: アカツクシガモ
  cn:赤麻鸭
Tadorna ferruginea

  www.avitopia.net/bird.en/?vid=201501

Photo W.J.Daunicht

adult

AU

Cotton Pygmy Goose
  de:Koromandelzwergente
  fr: Anserelle de Coromandel
  es:Gansito Asiático
  ja: ナンキンオシ
  cn:棉凫
Nettapus coromandelianus

Photo W.J.Daunicht

♂ adult

S2.0

Garganey
  de:Knäkente
  fr: Sarcelle d'été
  es:Cerceta Carretona
  ja: シマアジ
  cn:白眉鸭
Spatula querquedula

  www.avitopia.net/bird.en/?vid=203001
  www.avitopia.net/bird.en/?wid=203001

Photo Ferran Pestana

♂ adult

AU

Northern Shoveler
  de:Löffelente
  fr: Canard souchet
  es:Cuchara Común
  ja: ハシビロガモ
  cn:琵嘴鸭
Spatula clypeata

  www.avitopia.net/bird.en/?vid=203010
  www.avitopia.net/bird.en/?wid=203010

Photo W.J.Daunicht

Gadwall

de:Schnatterente
fr: Canard chipeau
es: Anade Friso
ja: オカヨシガモ
cn:赤膀鸭
Mareca strepera

www.avitopia.net/bird.en/?vid=203101

♂ adult

Photo D.Dewhurst

PD

Falcated Duck

de:Sichelente
fr: Canard à faucilles
es: Cerceta de Alfanjes
ja: ヨシガモ
cn:罗纹鸭
Mareca falcata
Near threatened.

♂ adult

Photo W.J.Daunicht

AU

Eurasian Wigeon

de:Pfeifente
fr: Canard siffleur
es: Silbón Europeo
ja: ヒドリガモ
cn:赤颈鸭
Mareca penelope

www.avitopia.net/bird.en/?vid=203103

♂ adult

Photo W.J.Daunicht

AU

Indian Spot-billed Duck

de:Fleckschnabelente
fr: Canard à bec tacheté
es: Pato Australiano
ja: カルガモ
cn:斑嘴鸭
Anas poecilorhyncha

adult

Photo W.J.Daunicht

AU

Photo DickDaniels

adult

Eastern Spot-billed Duck
de:Chinesiche Fleckschnabelente
fr: Canard de Chine
es:Pato Chino
ja: ヒガシカルガモ
cn:斑嘴鸭
Anas zonorhyncha

www.avitopia.net/bird.en/?vid=203209

Photo W.J.Daunicht

♂ adult

Mallard
de:Stockente
fr: Canard colvert
es: Ánade Real
ja: マガモ
cn:绿头鸭
Anas platyrhynchos

www.avitopia.net/bird.en/?vid=203210
www.avitopia.net/bird.en/?aud=203210

Photo D.Menke

♂ adult

Northern Pintail
de:Spießente
fr: Canard pilet
es: Ánade Rabudo
ja: オナガガモ
cn:针尾鸭
Anas acuta

www.avitopia.net/bird.en/?vid=203216

Photo W.J.Daunicht

♂ adult

Green-winged Teal
de:Krickente
fr: Sarcelle d'hiver
es:Cerceta común
ja: コガモ
cn:绿翅鸭
Anas crecca

www.avitopia.net/bird.en/?vid=203219

White-winged Duck
 de: Weißflügel-Moschusente
 fr: Canard à ailes blanches
 es: Pato de Jungla
 ja: ハジロモリガモ
 cn: 白翅栖鸭
Asarcornis scutulata
Endangered.

adult

Common Pochard
 de: Tafelente
 fr: Fuligule milouin
 es: Porrón Europeo
 ja: ホシハジロ
 cn: 红头潜鸭
Aythya ferina
Vulnerable.

www.avitopia.net/bird.en/?vid=203803

♂ adult

Baer's Pochard
 de: Baermoorente
 fr: Fuligule de Baer
 es: Porrón de Baer
 ja: アカハジロ
 cn: 青头潜鸭
Aythya baeri
Critically endangered.

adult

Tufted Duck
 de: Reiherente
 fr: Fuligule morillon
 es: Porrón Moñudo
 ja: キンクロハジロ
 cn: 凤头潜鸭
Aythya fuligula

www.avitopia.net/bird.en/?vid=203809

♂ adult

Red-breasted Merganser
de:Mittelsäger
fr: Harle huppé
es:Serreta Mediana
ja:ウミアイサ
cn:红胸秋沙鸭
Mergus serrator

Photo W.J.Daunicht

♂ adult

Pheasants - *Phasianidae*

The pheasant family is distributed worldwide, with the exception of northern Asia, southern South America and the polar regions. The lengths are very different and range from 13 cm to 2 m. They all have round wings, short necks and short thick beaks. The plumage is often very conspicuously patterned and the sexes are mostly different. Most pheasants live on the ground, but some species sleep in trees.

Hill Partridge
de:Hügelhuhn
fr: Torquéole à collier
es: Arborófila Común
ja:チャガシラミヤマテッケイ
cn:环颈山鹧鸪
Arborophila torqueola

Drawing Pretre

♂ adult

Rufous-throated Partridge
de:Rotkehl-Buschwachtel
fr: Torquéole à gorge rousse
es: Arborófila Golirrufa
ja:ノドアカミヤマテッケイ
cn:红喉山鹧鸪
Arborophila rufogularis

Photo JJ Harrison

adult

Bar-backed Partridge
 de:Braunbrust-Buschwachtel
 fr: Torquéole à poitrine brune
 es: Arborófila Pechiparda
 ja: チャムネミヤマテッケイ
 cn:褐胸山鹧鸪
Arborophila brunneopectus

adult

Orange-necked Partridge
 de:Davidbuschwachtel
 fr: Torquéole de David
 es: Arborófila de David
 ja: サイゴンミヤマテッケイ
 cn:橙颈山鹧鸪
Arborophila davidi
Endemic.
Near threatened.

adult

Green-legged Partridge
 de:Grünfuß-Buschwachtel
 fr: Torquéole des bois
 es: Arborófila Pativerde
 ja: アオアシミヤマテッケイ
 cn:绿脚山鹧鸪
Arborophila chloropus

adult

Crested Argus
 de:Perlenfasan
 fr: Argus ocellé
 es: Argos Perlado
 ja: カンムリセイラン
 cn:冠眼斑雉
Rheinardia ocellata
Near threatened.

♂♀ adult

♂ adult

AU

Green Peafowl
de:Ährenträgerpfau
fr: Paon spicifère
es: Pavo-real Cuelliverde
ja: マクジャク
cn:绿孔雀
Pavo muticus
Endangered.

Photo W.J.Daunicht

adult, pullus

PD

Germain's Peacock-Pheasant
de:Brauner Pfaufasan
fr: Éperonnier de Germain
es: Espolonero de Germain
ja: カッショクコクジャク
cn:眼斑孔雀雉
Polyplectron germaini
Endemic.
Near threatened.

Drawing J.Wolf

♂♀ adult

PD

Grey Peacock-Pheasant
de:Grauer Pfaufasan
fr: Éperonnier chinquis
es: Espolonero Chinquis
ja: コクジャク
cn:灰孔雀雉
Polyplectron bicalcaratum

Drawing J.Gould&H.C.Richter

♂

AU

King Quail
de:Zwergwachtel
fr: Caille peinte
es: Codorniz China
ja: ヒメウズラ
cn:蓝胸鹑
Synoicus chinensis

www.avitopia.net/bird.en/?vid=326502

Photo W.J.Daunicht

Japanese Quail
de: Japanwachtel
fr: Caille du Japon
es: Codorniz Japonesa
ja: ウズラ
cn: 鹌鹑

Coturnix japonica
Near threatened.

www.avitopia.net/bird.en/?vid=326801

adab

Photo W.J.Daunicht

AU

adult

Common Quail
de: Wachtel
fr: Caille des blés
es: Codorniz Común
ja: ヨアロッパウズラ
cn: 西鹌鹑

Coturnix coturnix

www.avitopia.net/bird.en/?vid=326802

S3.0

Photo Phi.Ju

♀ adult

Chinese Francolin
de: Perlfrankolin
fr: Francolin perlé
es: Francolín Chino
ja: コモンシャコ
cn: 中华鹧鸪

Francolinus pintadeanus

PD

Drawing W.J.Swainson

♂ adult

Mountain Bamboo Partridge
de: Gelbbrauen-Bambushuhn
fr: Bambusicole de Fytch
es: Bambusícola Montana
ja: ウンナンコジュケイ
cn: 棕胸竹鸡

Bambusicola fytchii

PD

Drawing J.Smit

adult

♂ adult

AU

Red Junglefowl
  de:Bankivahuhn
  fr: Coq bankiva
  es:Gallo Bankiva
  ja:セキショクヤケイ
  cn:原鸡
Gallus gallus

www.avitopia.net/bird.en/?vid=327701
www.avitopia.net/bird.en/?aud=327701

Photo W.J.Daunicht

♂ adult

AU

Temminck's Tragopan
  de:Temmincktragopan
  fr: Tragopan de Temminck
  es:Tragopán Cariazul
  ja:ベニジュケイ
  cn:红腹角雉
Tragopan temminckii

Photo W.J.Daunicht

♂ adult

AU

Lady Amherst's Pheasant
  de:Diamantfasan
  fr: Faisan de Lady Amherst
  es:Faisán de Lady Amherst
  ja:ギンケイ
  cn:白腹锦鸡
Chrysolophus amherstiae

Photo W.J.Daunicht

♂ adult

AU

Common Pheasant
  de:Fasan
  fr: Faisan de Colchide
  es:Faisán Vulgar
  ja:キジ
  cn:环颈雉
Phasianus colchicus

www.avitopia.net/bird.en/?kom=328701
www.avitopia.net/bird.en/?vid=328701
www.avitopia.net/bird.en/?aud=328701

Photo W.J.Daunicht

Silver Pheasant
de:Silberfasan
fr: Faisan argenté
es: Faisán Plateado
ja: ハッカン
cn:白鷴
Lophura nycthemera

♂ adult

Siamese Fireback
de:Prälatfasan
fr: Faisan prélat
es: Faisán Siamés
ja: シマハッカン
cn:戴氏火背鷴
Lophura diardi

adult

Edwards's Pheasant
de:Edwardsfasan
fr: Faisan d'Edwards
es: Faisán de Eduardo
ja: コサンケイ
cn:爱氏鷴
Lophura edwardsi
Endemic.
Critically endangered.

 www.avitopia.net/bird.en/?vid=329005

♂ adult

Grebes - *Podicipedidae*

The family of Grebes are found on freshwater lakes around the world, except in the extreme north and south and on some islands. In winter they can also be found on the coast of the sea. The size ranges from 20 cm to 50 cm, the wings are short, tail feathers are missing. The toes have flap-like widenings. They only fly regularly and at night during the migration time. In addition, they are well adapted to aquatic life. Both parents lead the striped or spotted young birds until they become independent.

AU

Photo W.J.Daunicht

breeding

Little Grebe
de:Zwergtaucher
fr: Grèbe castagneux
es:Zampullín Común
ja: カイツブリ
cn:小鸊鷉
Tachybaptus ruficollis

🔊 www.avitopia.net/bird.en/?kom=375202
🎞 www.avitopia.net/bird.en/?vid=375202

AU

Photo W.J.Daunicht

breeding

Great Crested Grebe
de:Haubentaucher
fr: Grèbe huppé
es:Somormujo Lavanco
ja: カンムリカイツブリ
cn:凤头鸊鷉
Podiceps cristatus

🎞 www.avitopia.net/bird.en/?vid=375504
🎞 www.avitopia.net/bird.en/?wid=375504

Petrels - *Procellariidae*

The family of Petrels is at home at sea all over the world. They essentially use the land for breeding, and some species even do so on the coast of Antarctica. Most of the species are migratory birds. The body length ranges from 30 cm to 90 cm. The birds have long, pointed wings and short tails, and their feet are webbed. The smaller species breed in caves or crevices, they defend the young birds by vomiting stinking oil.

Bulwer's Petrel
 de:Bulwersturmvogel
 fr: Pétrel de Bulwer
 es:Petrel de Bulwer
 ja: アナドリ
 cn:褐燕鸌
Bulweria bulwerii

adult

Wedge-tailed Shearwater
 de:Keilschwanz-Sturmtaucher
 fr: Puffin fouquet
 es:Pardela del Pacífico
 ja: オナガミズナギドリ
 cn:曳尾鸌
Ardenna pacifica

adult

Short-tailed Shearwater
 de:Kurzschwanz-Sturmtaucher
 fr: Puffin à bec grêle
 es:Pardela de Tasmania
 ja: ハシボソミズナギドリ
 cn:短尾鸌
Ardenna tenuirostris

adult

Storm-petrels - *Hydrobatidae*

The family of Storm-petrels is widespread on all oceans of the earth and occurs partly in large numbers. With a body length of 14 cm to 25 cm, they are the smallest seabirds with webbed feet. Your weak legs are hardly able to carry their body weight without the support of the wings. They breed in colonies in caves or crevices, which they usually only attend at night. Although they usually breed on mammal-free islands, the greatest danger comes from introduced mammals. The Guadalupe storm-petrel was driven to extinction by feral cats.

adult

Drawing J.G.Keulemans

PD Wilson's Storm Petrel
de:Buntfuß-Sturmschwalbe
fr: Océanite de Wilson
es: Paíño de Wilson
ja: アシナガウミツバメ
cn:黄蹼洋海燕
Oceanites oceanicus

adult

Drawing J.Smit

PD Swinhoe's Storm Petrel
de:Swinhoewellenläufer
fr: Océanite de Swinhoe
es: Paíño de Swinhoe
ja: ヒメクロウミツバメ
cn:黑叉尾海燕
Oceanodroma monorhis
Near threatened.

Storks - *Ciconiidae*

The family of storks is widespread worldwide except for the coldest areas. Some species are resident birds, others are long-distance migrants. The body length ranges from 75 cm to 150 cm. They are long-legged birds with large wings, a long neck and a long beak. They fly a lot, usually with a stretched neck, and they sail excellently. They feed on small animals, from insects to small mammals. 3 to 6 eggs are laid in the shallow nest made of brushwood, which are incubated by both parents.

Asian Openbill
 de:Silberklaffschnabel
 fr: Bec-ouvert indien
 es: Picotenaza Asiático
 ja: スキハシコウ
 cn: 钳嘴鹳
Anastomus oscitans

adult

Black Stork
 de:Schwarzstorch
 fr: Cigogne noire
 es: Cigüeña Negra
 ja: ナベコウ
 cn: 黑鹳
Ciconia nigra

www.avitopia.net/bird.en/?vid=550201

adult

Woolly-necked Stork
 de:Wollhalsstorch
 fr: Cigogne épiscopale
 es: Cigüeña Lanuda
 ja: エンビコウ
 cn: 白颈鹳
Ciconia episcopus
Vulnerable.

www.avitopia.net/bird.en/?vid=550203

adult

Photo Pierre de Chabannes

Photo W.J.Daunicht

Photo W.J.Daunicht

Photo W.J.Daunicht

AU

σ adult

Black-necked Stork
de:Riesenstorch
fr: Jabiru d'Asie
es: Jabirú Asiático
ja: セイタカコウ
cn:黑颈鹳
Ephippiorhynchus asiaticus
Near threatened.

Photo Koshy Koshy

A2.0

adult

Lesser Adjutant
de:Kleiner Adjutant
fr: Marabout chevelu
es: Marabú Menor
ja: コハゲコウ
cn:秃鹳
Leptoptilos javanicus
Vulnerable.

Photo Yathin SK

A2.5

adult

Greater Adjutant
de:Großer Adjutant
fr: Marabout argala
es: Marabú Argala
ja: オオハゲコウ
cn:大秃鹳
Leptoptilos dubius
Endangered.

Drawing Huet

PD

σ adult

Milky Stork
de:Milchstorch
fr: Tantale blanc
es: Tántalo Malayo
ja: シロトキコウ
cn:白鹮鹳
Mycteria cinerea
Endangered.

Painted Stork
  de:Buntstorch
  fr: Tantale indien
  es:Tántalo Indio
  ja: インドトキコウ
  cn:彩鹳
Mycteria leucocephala
Near threatened.

adult

Frigate-birds - *Fregatidae*

The family of Frigate-birds can be found at all tropical and subtropical seas. Their length ranges from 80 cm to 105 cm. They have very long wings, a curved beak, and a forked tail. The males have a scarlet throat pouch during the breeding season, which is inflated during courtship. They feed on fish, but never go down on the water, instead catch them in flight. Frigate birds often parasitize other birds by chasing them until they regurgitate their food. The nest can reach a diameter of 4.5 m. The single egg is incubated by both adult birds for 40 days. The chick is fledged after 4 to 5 months.

Lesser Frigatebird
  de:Arielfregattvogel
  fr: Frégate ariel
  es:Rabihorcado Chico
  ja: コグンカンドリ
  cn:白斑军舰鸟
Fregata ariel

♂ adult

Christmas Frigatebird
  de:Weißbauch-Fregattvogel
  fr: Frégate d'Andrews
  es:Rabihorcado de la Christmas
  ja: シロハラグンカンドリ
  cn:白腹军舰鸟
Fregata andrewsi
Critically endangered.

♂♀ adult

Great Frigatebird
de:Bindenfregattvogel
fr: Frégate du Pacifique
es: Rabihorcado Grande
ja: オオグンカンドリ
cn:黑腹军舰鸟
Fregata minor

♂ adult

Photo Jason Corriveau

Gannets, Boobies - *Sulidae*

The family of Boobies is common on all seas near the coast. The birds are 65 cm to 100 cm long. The wings are long and pointed, the legs are short and the feet are large and webbed. The beak is strong and has no nostrils. Boobies are extremely elegant fliers, but quite awkward on the ground. They hunt fish for which they plunge into water from a height of up to 35 m in order to pursue them under water and to grab them with their beak. They breed in colonies on the ground or on trees. The young birds are provided with regurgitated food.

Masked Booby
de:Maskentölpel
fr: Fou masqué
es: Alcatraz Enmascarado
ja: アオツラカツオドリ
cn:蓝脸鲣鸟
Sula dactylatra

adult

Photo R.Graf

Brown Booby
de:Weißbauchtölpel
fr: Fou brun
es: Piquero Pardo
ja: カツオドリ
cn:褐鲣鸟
Sula leucogaster

adult

Photo USGS Unmanned Aircraft System

Red-footed Booby
de: Rotfußtölpel
fr: Fou à pieds rouges
es: Piquero Patirrojo
ja: アカアシカツオドリ
cn: 红脚鲣鸟
Sula sula

S3.0

Photo Charlesjsharp

♂ adult

Cormorants - *Phalacrocoracidae*

The cormorant family are gregarious freshwater or marine birds found on every continent. The body length is 50 cm to 100 cm. They have short legs with large webbed feet. They have a long neck and a slender beak with a curved tip. They dive from the surface of the water and can stay underwater for minutes. The caught fish are thrown into the air and devoured head first.

Little Cormorant
de: Mohrenscharbe
fr: Cormoran de Vieillot
es: Cormorán de Java
ja: アジアコビトウ
cn: 黑颈鸬鹚
Microcarbo niger

S3.0

Photo J.M.Garg

adult

Great Cormorant
de: Kormoran
fr: Grand Cormoran
es: Cormorán Grande
ja: カワウ
cn: 普通鸬鹚
Phalacrocorax carbo

www.avitopia.net/bird.en/?vid=625206

LIC

Photo W.D.G.Daunicht

breeding

Photo J.J.Harrison

S3.0

Indian Cormorant
  de:Braunwangenscharbe
  fr: Cormoran à cou brun
  es:Cormorán Indio
  ja:インドヒメウ
  cn:印度鸬鹚
Phalacrocorax fuscicollis

adult

Darters (Anhingas) - *Anhingidae*

The family of Darters occurs in the tropics and subtropics of all continents. The northern populations are migratory birds. The body size is 90 cm. The birds have long wings, a long trunk and tail. The legs are short, the large feet are webbed. The head is small and the neck and pointed beak are long and slender. They use their pointed beak to spear fish when hunting underwater. They cannot grease their feathers, so they soak up water and have to be dried with outstretched wings. Darters nest in colonies often in the company of other water birds. The male chooses the nesting site and carries branches that the female uses to build the nest.

Drawing W.J.Daunicht

AU

Oriental Darter
  de:Indischer Schlangenhalsvogel
  fr: Anhinga orientale
  es: Anhinga Oriental
  ja:アジアヘビウ
  cn:黑腹蛇鹈
Anhinga melanogaster
Near threatened.

♂ adult

Pelicans - *Pelecanidae*

The family of Pelicans is scattered across all continents. The body length is 125 cm to 180 cm. The legs are short and strong, the toes are webbed. The wings are large, the tail is short, and the birds sail excellently. The beak is long, straight and flat, and at the lower part of the beak is a large, stretchy pouch that is used like a fishing net. Pelicans are very sociable and often work together to fish. Some species plunge into the water from great heights. Pelicans nest in colonies.

Spot-billed Pelican
  de:Graupelikan
  fr: Pélican à bec tacheté
  es:Pelícano Oriental
  ja:ハイイロペリカン
  cn:斑嘴鹈鹕
Pelecanus philippensis
Near threatened.

adult

Herons - *Ardeidae*

The family of Herons occurs on all continents and on many islands. The body length ranges from 28 nm to 140 cm. The wings are large, the tail is short. Legs, toes and neck are long, the latter has a characteristic S-shape. They feed mainly on fish, but also eat other small animals. They mostly breed in colonies. The food brought in is regurgitated in front of the chicks.

Yellow Bittern
  de:Chinadommel
  fr: Blongios de Chine
  es:Avetorillo Chino
  ja:ヨシゴイ
  cn:黄斑苇鳽
Ixobrychus sinensis

♂ breeding

Von Schrenck's Bittern
  de:Mandschurendommel
  fr: Blongios de Schrenck
  es:Avetorillo Manchú
  ja:オオヨシゴイ
  cn:紫背苇鳽
Ixobrychus eurhythmus

♂ adult

adult

PD **Cinnamon Bittern**
de:Zimtdommel
fr: Blongios cannelle
es: Avetorillo Canelo
ja: リュウキュウヨシゴイ
cn:栗苇鳽
Ixobrychus cinnamomeus

Drawing H.Groenvold

adult

PD **Black Bittern**
de:Schwarzdommel
fr: Blongios à cou jaune
es: Avetorillo Negro
ja: タカサゴクロサギ
cn:黑苇鳽
Ixobrychus flavicollis

Drawing J.Smit

adult

AU **Grey Heron**
de:Graureiher
fr: Héron cendré
es: Garza Real
ja: アオサギ
cn:苍鹭
Ardea cinerea

www.avitopia.net/bird.en/?vid=750702
www.avitopia.net/bird.en/?wid=750702

Photo W.J.Daunicht

juvenile

AU **Great-billed Heron**
de:Rußreiher
fr: Héron typhon
es: Garza de Sumatra
ja: スマトラサギ
cn:大嘴鹭
Ardea sumatrana

Photo W.J.Daunicht

Purple Heron
  de:Purpurreiher
  fr: Héron pourpré
  es: Garza Imperial
  ja: ムラサキサギ
  cn:草鷺
Ardea purpurea

  www.avitopia.net/bird.en/?vid=750710

AU

Photo W.J.Daunicht

adult

Great Egret
  de:Silberreiher
  fr: Grande Aigrette
  es: Garceta Grande
  ja: ダイサギ
  cn:大白鷺
Ardea alba

  www.avitopia.net/bird.en/?vid=750711
  www.avitopia.net/bird.en/?wid=750711

AU

Photo W.J.Daunicht

adult

Yellow-billed Egret
  de:Mittelreiher
  fr: Héron intermédiaire
  es: Garceta Intermedia
  ja: チュウサギ
  cn:中白鷺
Ardea intermedia

AU

Photo W.J.Daunicht

adult

Chinese Egret
  de:Schneereiher
  fr: Aigrette de Chine
  es: Garceta China
  ja: カラシラサギ
  cn:黄嘴白鷺
Egretta eulophotes
Vulnerable.

S4.0

Photo Morton Strange

adult

Photo W.J.Daunicht

breeding

AU

Little Egret

  de:Seidenreiher
  fr: Aigrette garzette
  es: Garceta Común
  ja: コサギ
  cn:白鷺

Egretta garzetta

www.avitopia.net/bird.en/?vid=750803

Photo W.J.Daunicht

adult, dark phase

AU

Pacific Reef Heron

  de:Riffreiher
  fr: Aigrette sacrée
  es: Garceta de Arrecife
  ja: クロサギ
  cn:岩鷺

Egretta sacra

Photo W.J.Daunicht

breeding

AU

Cattle Egret

  de:Kuhreiher
  fr: Héron garde-boeufs
  es: Garcilla Bueyera
  ja: アマサギ
  cn:牛背鷺

Bubulcus ibis

www.avitopia.net/bird.en/?vid=750901

Photo Lip Kee Yap

non-breeding

S2.0

Chinese Pond Heron

  de:Bacchusreiher
  fr: Crabier chinois
  es: Garcilla China
  ja: アカガシラサギ
  cn:池鷺

Ardeola bacchus

Javan Pond Heron
 de:Prachtreiher
 fr: Crabier malais
 es: Garcilla Indonesia
 ja: ジャワアカガシラサギ
 cn:爪哇池鹭
Ardeola speciosa

www.avitopia.net/bird.en/?vid=751004

breeding

Striated Heron
 de:Mangrovereiher
 fr: Héron strié
 es: Garcita Azulada
 ja: ササゴイ
 cn:小绿鹭
Butorides striata

www.avitopia.net/bird.en/?vid=751102

adult

Black-crowned Night Heron
 de:Nachtreiher
 fr: Bihoreau gris
 es: Martinete Común
 ja: ゴイサギ
 cn:夜鹭
Nycticorax nycticorax

www.avitopia.net/bird.en/?vid=751501

breeding

White-eared Night Heron
 de:Hainanreiher
 fr: Bihoreau superbe
 es: Martinete Magnífico
 ja: ハイナンミゾゴイ
 cn:海南鳽
Gorsachius magnificus
Endangered.

adult

Drawing H.Groenvold

adult, immature

PD Malayan Night Heron
de:Wellenreiher
fr: Bihoreau malais
es:Martinete Malayo
ja: ズグロミゾゴイ
cn:黑冠鳽
Gorsachius melanolophus

Ibises - *Threskiornithidae*

The family of Ibises occurs in all warm regions of the world. The birds are 50 cm to 110 cm high. They have long wings and a short tail. The toes are connected by small webs. The long beak is either curved downwards or broad and spatulate. Most species are quite gregarious. They fly powerfully and can sail with the neck stretched out. Their food is very varied. The Sacred Ibis was the revered symbol of the god Thoth in ancient Egypt, but is now extinct in this country.

Photo W.J.Daunicht

adult

AU Glossy Ibis
de:Sichler
fr: Ibis falcinelle
es:Morito Común
ja: ブロンズトキ
cn:彩鹮
Plegadis falcinellus

www.avitopia.net/bird.en/?vid=775201

Drawing Huet

adult

PD Black-headed Ibis
de:Schwarzhalsibis
fr: Ibis à tête noire
es:Ibis Oriental
ja: クロトキ
cn:黑头白鹮
Threskiornis melanocephalus
Near threatened.

www.avitopia.net/bird.en/?vid=775803

White-shouldered Ibis
de:Weißschulteribis
fr: Ibis de Davison
es:Ibis de Davison
ja: アカアシトキ
cn:白肩黑鹮
Pseudibis davisoni
Critically endangered.

adult

Giant Ibis
de:Riesenibis
fr: Ibis géant
es:Ibis Gigante
ja: オニアカアシトキ
cn:巨鹮
Pseudibis gigantea
Critically endangered.

adult

Black-faced Spoonbill
de:Schwarzgesichtlöffler
fr: Petite Spatule
es:Espátula Menor
ja: クロツラヘラサギ
cn:黑脸琵鹭
Platalea minor
Endangered.

non-breeding

Ospreys - *Pandionidae*

There is only one species in the family of ospreys, but it is a true cosmopolitan: it occurs on all continents. The birds are around 60 cm tall with long wings and short tails. The beak is hook-shaped and the feet have warty sole pads. Fischdler are pure fish hunters who hover first and then plunges into the water, often submerging themselves completely. The fish are grasped with the claws and carried to a sitting site or a nest. The female breeds and cares for the young birds alone.

AU

Osprey
> de:Fischadler
> fr: Balbuzard pêcheur
> es:Águila Pescadora
> ja: ミサゴ
> cn:鹗
> *Pandion haliaetus*

Photo W.J.Daunicht

♀ adult

Birds of Prey - *Accipitridae*

The family of Birds of Prey is found worldwide with the exception of the Arctic, Antarctic and most of the oceanic islands. Birds of Prey are of various sizes (20 - 115 cm), they have long, round wings, curved claws and a short hooked bill. The sexes are almost the same, the female is almost always larger. All species are good fliers, and many sail well too. They mainly hunt live animals, only the vultures are scavengers. Even fishing species are among them.

AU

Black-winged Kite
> de:Gleitaar
> fr:Élanion blanc
> es:Elanio Común
> ja: カタグロトビ
> cn:黑翅鸢
> *Elanus caeruleus*

www.avitopia.net/bird.en/?vid=875201

Photo W.J.Daunicht

adult

Crested Honey Buzzard
de:Schopfwespenbussard
fr: Bondrée orientale
es: Abejero Oriental
ja: ハチクマ
cn:凤头蜂鹰
Pernis ptilorhynchus

♂ adult

Jerdon's Baza
de:Hinduweih
fr: Baza de Jerdon
es: Baza Oriental
ja: チャイロカッコウハヤブサ
cn:褐冠鹃隼
Aviceda jerdoni

adult

Black Baza
de:Dreifarbenweih
fr: Baza huppard
es: Baza Negro
ja: クロカッコウハヤブサ
cn:黑冠鹃隼
Aviceda leuphotes

adult

Red-headed Vulture
de:Kahlkopfgeier
fr: Vautour royal
es: Buitre Cabecirrojo
ja: ミミハゲワシ
cn:黑兀鹫
Sarcogyps calvus
Critically endangered.

adult

immature

adult

adult

adult

PD White-rumped Vulture
de:Bengalengeier
fr: Vautour chaugoun
es:Buitre Dorsiblanco Bengalí
ja:ベンガルハゲワシ
cn:白背兀鷲
Gyps bengalensis
Critically endangered.

Drawing Huet

PD Slender-billed Vulture
de:Dünnschnabelgeier
fr: Vautour à bec élancé
es:Buitre Picofino
ja:ハシボソハゲワシ
cn:细嘴兀鷲
Gyps tenuirostris
Critically endangered.

Drawing D.W.Mitchell

PD Crested Serpent Eagle
de:Schlangenweihe
fr: Serpentaire bacha
es: Águila Culebrera Chiíla
ja: ミナミカンムリワシ
cn:蛇
Spilornis cheela

Drawing L.Reinold

AU Changeable Hawk-Eagle
de:Asiatischer Haubenadler
fr: Aigle variable
es: Águila-azor variable asiatica
ja: カワリクマタカ
cn:凤头鹰雕
Nisaetus limnaeetus

Photo W.J.Daunicht

Mountain Hawk-Eagle

de:Bergadler
fr: Aigle montagnard
es: Águila-azor Montañesa
ja: クマタカ
cn:鷹雕

Nisaetus nipalensis

adult

Drawing J.Wolf

PD

Rufous-bellied Eagle

de:Rotbauchadler
fr: Aigle à ventre roux
es: Águila-azor Ventrirroja
ja: アカハラクマタカ
cn:棕腹隼雕

Lophotriorchis kienerii

adult

Drawing G.S

PD

Black Eagle

de:Malaienadler
fr: Aigle noir
es: Águila Milana
ja: カザノワシ
cn:林雕

Ictinaetus malaiensis

adult

Drawing J.Smit

PD

Greater Spotted Eagle

de:Schelladler
fr: Aigle criard
es: Águila Moteada
ja: カラフトワシ
cn:乌雕

Clanga clanga
Vulnerable.

adult

Photo J.M.Garg

S3.0

adult

PD **Asian Imperial Eagle**
  de:Kaiseradler
  fr: Aigle impérial
  es:Águila Imperial Oriental
  ja:カタジロワシ
  cn:白肩雕
  Aquila heliaca
  Vulnerable.

Drawing C.R.Bree

♂ adult

PD **Bonelli's Eagle**
  de:Habichtsadler
  fr: Aigle de Bonelli
  es:Águila perdicera
  ja:ボネリアクマタカ
  cn:白腹隼雕
  Aquila fasciata

Drawing J.G.Keulemans

♂ adult

PD **Rufous-winged Buzzard**
  de:Malaienteesa
  fr: Busautour pâle
  es:Busardo Alirrufo
  ja:チャバネサシバ
  cn:棕翅鵟鹰
  Butastur liventer

Drawing Huet

S3.0 **Grey-faced Buzzard**
  de:Kifernteesa
  fr: Busautour à joues grises
  es:Busardo Carigrís
  ja:サシバ
  cn:灰脸鵟鹰
  Butastur indicus

Photo M.Nishimura

adult

Eastern Marsh Harrier
  de:Mangroveweihe
  fr: Busard d'Orient
  es: Aguilucho Lagunero Oriental
  ja: チュウヒ
  cn:白腹鹞
Circus spilonotus

♀ adult

Northern Harrier
  de:Kornweihe
  fr: Busard Saint-Martin
  es: Aguilucho Pálido
  ja: ハイイロチュウヒ
  cn:白尾鹞
Circus cyaneus

  www.avitopia.net/bird.en/?vid=880110

♂ adult

Pied Harrier
  de:Elsterweihe
  fr: Busard tchoug
  es: Aguilucho Pío
  ja: マダラチュウヒ
  cn:鹊鹞
Circus melanoleucos

♂ adult

Crested Goshawk
  de:Schopfhabicht
  fr: Autour huppé
  es: Azor Moñudo
  ja: カンムリオオタカ
  cn:凤头鹰
Accipiter trivirgatus

adult

adult

AU **Shikra**
  de: Schikra
  fr: Épervier shikra
  es: Gavilán Chikra
  ja: タカサゴタカ
  cn: 褐耳鹰
  Accipiter badius

♀ adult

PD **Chinese Sparrowhawk**
  de: Froschsperber
  fr: Épervier de Horsfield
  es: Gavilán Ranero
  ja: アカハラダカ
  cn: 赤腹鹰
  Accipiter soloensis

♂♀ adult

PD **Japanese Sparrowhawk**
  de: Trillersperber
  fr: Épervier du Japon
  es: Gavilancito Japonés
  ja: ツミ
  cn: 日本松雀鹰
  Accipiter gularis

adult

PD **Besra**
  de: Besrasperber
  fr: Épervier besra
  es: Gavilán Besra
  ja: ミナミツミ
  cn: 松雀鹰
  Accipiter virgatus

Eurasian Sparrowhawk
de:Sperber
fr: Épervier d'Europe
es: Gavilán Común
ja: ハイタカ
cn:雀鷹
Accipiter nisus

♀ adult

Northern Goshawk
de:Habicht
fr: Autour des palombes
es: Azor Común
ja: オオタカ
cn:苍鹰
Accipiter gentilis

adult

Black Kite
de:Schwarzmilan
fr: Milan noir
es: Milano Negro
ja: トビ
cn:黑鸢
Milvus migrans

www.avitopia.net/bird.en/?vid=880602

adult

Brahminy Kite
de:Brahminenweih
fr: Milan sacré
es: Milano Brahmán
ja: シロガシラトビ
cn:栗鸢
Haliastur indus

adult

adult

AU

White-tailed Eagle
de:Seeadler
fr: Pygargue à queue blanche
es: Pigargo Europeo
ja: オジロワシ
cn:白尾海雕

Haliaeetus albicilla

www.avitopia.net/bird.en/?vid=880802

Photo W.J.Daunicht

adult

AU

White-bellied Sea Eagle
de:Weißbauch-Seeadler
fr: Pygargue blagre
es: Pigargo Oriental
ja: シロハラウミワシ
cn:白腹海雕

Haliaeetus leucogaster

Photo W.J.Daunicht

adult

PD

Lesser Fish Eagle
de:Braunschwanz-Seeadler
fr: Pygargue nain
es: Pigarguillo Menor
ja: コウオクイワシ
cn:魚雕

Haliaeetus humilis
Near threatened.

Drawing J.Smit

adult

S2.0

Grey-headed Fish Eagle
de:Graukopf-Seeadler
fr: Pygargue à tête grise
es: Pigarguillo Común
ja: ウオクイワシ
cn:灰头鱼雕

Haliaeetus ichthyaetus
Near threatened.

Photo Lip Kee Yap

Common Buzzard

de: Mäusebussard
fr: Buse variable
es: Busardo Ratonero
ja: ノスリ
cn: 普通鵟

Buteo buteo

www.avitopia.net/bird.en/?vid=881816
www.avitopia.net/bird.en/?aud=881816

AU

Photo W.J.Daunicht

adult

Himalayan Buzzard

de: Tibetbussard
fr: Buse de l'Himalaya
es: Busardo del Himalaya
ja: ヒマラヤノスリ
cn: 喜山鵟

Buteo refectus

S4.0

Photo Dibyendu Ash

adult

Japanese Buzzard

de: Japanbussard
fr: Buse du Japon
es: Busardo japonés
ja: ノスリ
cn: 普通鵟

Buteo japonicus

PD

Drawing J.G.Keulemans

adult

Bustards - *Otididae*

The family of Bustards occurs in Africa, Eurasia and Australia. The height of the birds ranges from 38 cm to 130 cm. They have long broad wings, long strong legs with three short toes and a long neck. The beak is short, strong and flattened. Their habitat are free plains. They fly well, but are downright ground birds. All species are omnivorous. In courtship, the throat pouch serves to amplify the voice. The nest is an unpadded recess in the ground in which 1 to 5 eggs are laid. The young birds flee the nest.

PD Bengal Florican
   de:Barttrappe
   fr: Outarde du Bengale
   es: Sisón Bengalí
   ja:ベンガルショウノガン
   cn:南亚鸨
Houbaropsis bengalensis
Critically endangered.

Drawing H.Groenvold

♂♀ adult, juvenile

Rails, Waterhens, and Coots - *Rallidae*

The family of Rails and Coots occurs worldwide except in the polar regions. Rails are at most medium-sized birds (15 - 50 cm) with short wings and very short tails. The toes are long and have swimming lobes in the coots. The sexes usually look the same. Almost all species swim well. Many only become active at dusk or are night birds. Some are able to fly long distances, while island species are partially flightless.

PD Red-legged Crake
   de:Malaienralle
   fr: Râle barré
   es: Polluela Patirroja
   ja:ナンヨウオオクイナ
   cn:红腿斑秧鸡
Rallina fasciata

Drawing E.Neale

adult

Slaty-legged Crake
 de:Hinduralle
 fr: Râle de forêt
 es:Polluela de Jungla
 ja:オオクイナ
 cn:白喉斑秧鸡
Rallina eurizonoides

adult

Slaty-breasted Rail
 de:Graubrustralle
 fr: Râle strié
 es:Rascón Rufigrís
 ja:ミナミクイナ
 cn:灰胸秧鸡
Gallirallus striatus

adult

Brown-cheeked Rail
 de:Asienwasserralle
 fr: Râle à joues brunes
 es:Rascón asiático
 ja:クイナ
 cn:普通秧鸡
Rallus indicus

adult

White-breasted Waterhen
 de:Weißbrust-Kielralle
 fr: Râle à poitrine blanche
 es:Gallineta Pechiblanca
 ja:シロハラクイナ
 cn:白胸苦恶鸟
Amaurornis phoenicurus

adult

adult

Drawing J.G.Keulemans

PD

White-browed Crake
de: Weißbrauen-Sumpfhuhn
fr: Marouette grise
es: Polluela Cejiblanca
ja: マミジロクイナ
cn: 白眉田鸡
Amaurornis cinerea

adult

Photo J.M.Garg

S3.0

Ruddy-breasted Crake
de: Zimtsumpfhuhn
fr: Marouette brune
es: Polluela Pechirrufa
ja: ヒクイナ
cn: 红胸田鸡
Zapornia fusca

adult

Drawing H.Groenvold

PD

Band-bellied Crake
de: Mandarinsumpfhuhn
fr: Marouette mandarin
es: Polluela Mandarín
ja: コウライヒクイナ
cn: 斑胁田鸡
Zapornia paykullii
Near threatened.

adult

Drawing J.G.Keulemans

PD

Brown Bush-hen
de: Braunbauch-Kielralle
fr: Râle akool
es: Gallineta Akool
ja: チャバンネクイナ
cn: 红脚苦恶鸟
Zapornia akool

Baillon's Crake
  de:Zwergsumpfhuhn
  fr: Marouette de Baillon
  es: Polluela Chica
  ja: ヒメクイナ
  cn: 小田鸡
Zapornia pusilla

adult

Black-tailed Crake
  de:Zweifarben-Kielralle
  fr: Râle bicolore
  es: Polluela Bicolor
  ja: オグロクイナ
  cn: 黑尾苦恶鸟
Zapornia bicolor

adult

Watercock
  de:Wasserhahn
  fr: Râle à crête
  es: Gallineta Crestada
  ja: ツルクイナ
  cn: 董鸡
Gallicrex cinerea

♂ adult

Black-backed Swamphen
  de:Schwarzrücken-Purpurhuhn
  fr: Talève à dos noir
  es: Calamón de Lomo Negro
  ja: セグロセイケイ
  cn: 黑背紫水鸡
Porphyrio indicus

adult

adult

Photo W.J.Daunicht

AU

Common Moorhen

de:Teichhuhn
fr: Gallinule poule-d'eau
es: Gallereta Común
ja: バン
cn:黑水鸡

Gallinula chloropus

www.avitopia.net/bird.en/?kom=1003303
www.avitopia.net/bird.en/?vid=1003303

adult

Photo W.J.Daunicht

AU

Eurasian Coot

de:Blässhuhn
fr: Foulque macroule
es: Focha Común
ja: オオバン
cn:白骨顶

Fulica atra

www.avitopia.net/bird.en/?vid=1003506
www.avitopia.net/bird.en/?aud=1003506

Finfoots - *Heliornithidae*

The three types of the family of Finfoots occur in certain tropical and subtropical areas of the continents America, Africa and Asia. Their body length ranges from 30 cm to 60 cm. The legs are short and strong with long toes carrying wide swimming flaps. Their habitat are rivers, lakes and swamps. They swim excellently, are rather shy and solitary and defend their territory. Their diet consists mainly of invertebrates, but small vertebrates and little vegetarian food are also eaten. For the American Sungrebe it has been proven that the young are completely helpless after an incubation period of only 10 to 11 days, but can be transported by the male in a skin pocket under each wing. The Sungrebe is the only bird in the world that can even do this in flight.

Masked Finfoot
   de:Maskenbinsenralle
   fr: Grébifoulque d'Asie
   es: Avesol Asiático
   ja: アジアヒレアシ
   cn:亚洲鳍趾鹛
Heliopais personatus
Endangered.

adult

Cranes - *Gruidae*

The family of Cranes occurs worldwide except for South America. The body size ranges from 90 cm to 175 cm. They have long legs, necks, and beaks, but short tails. The inner arm feathers are converted into overhanging ornamental feathers. They owe their loud voice to an extension of the windpipe into the breastbone. They are excellent gliders who fly with their necks outstretched. They feed on a variety of animal and vegetable foods. They build their nests on the ground or even in water. The 2 or 3 eggs are incubated by both partners and both also look after the young birds who flee the nest.

Sarus Crane
   de:Saruskranich
   fr: Grue antigone
   es: Grulla Sarus
   ja: オオヅル
   cn:赤颈鹤
Antigone antigone
Vulnerable.

www.avitopia.net/bird.en/?vid=1125502

♂♀ adult

Thick-knees - *Burhinidae*

The family of Thick-knees occurs on every continent on earth. They are 36 cm to 52 cm long. They have fairly long wings and a half-length tail. The legs are long and the feet have three webbed toes. The head is thick with large eyes. They are twilight and night birds and some species are gregarious. They rarely fly and feed on various small animals. Two eggs are usually laid in the nests on the ground. Both parents breed and later look after the young.

A2.0

Photo Sumeet Moghe

adult

Indian Thick-knee
de:Indientriel
fr: Oedicnème indien
es: Alcaraván indio
ja:インドイシチドリ
cn:印度石鸻
Burhinus indicus

S3.0

Photo Thimindu

adult

Great Stone-curlew
de:Krabbentriel
fr: Grand Oedicnème
es: Alcaraván Picogrueso Indio
ja: ソリハシオオイシチドリ
cn:大石鸻
Esacus recurvirostris
Near threatened.

S4.0

Photo Charles Davies

adult

Beach Stone-curlew
de:Rifftriel
fr: Oedicnème des récifs
es: Alcaraván Picogrueso Australiano
ja:ハシブトオオイシチドリ
cn:澳洲石鸻
Esacus magnirostris
Near threatened.

Stilts and Avocets - *Recurvirostridae*

The family of Stilts and Avocets is widespread worldwide; the northern populations are migratory birds. The body length is 30 cm to 50 cm. They have very long legs and a thin beak that is straight or curved upwards. They fly well and can swim well. They search the mud in shallow waters for invertebrates. They nest in colonies, the nest-fleeing young birds are looked after by both parents. The defense of the offspring includes various distraction techniques from simulating a 'broken wing' to 'false brooding' in full view of a predator.

Black-winged Stilt
  de:Stelzenläufer
  fr: Échasse blanche
  es:Cigüeñuela de Alas Negras
  ja: セイタカシギ
  cn:黑翅长脚鹬
Himantopus himantopus

 www.avitopia.net/bird.en/?vid=1250101
 www.avitopia.net/bird.en/?aud=1250101

adult

Plovers - *Charadriidae*

The plover family is global; many species are migratory birds. The body length ranges from 15 cm to 40 cm. Plover have a stocky body and long wings, the hind toe is receded or missing completely. They are ground birds that can run quickly, but also fly very well and quickly. In the vicinity of the nest or the young birds, the adult birds use seduction by simulating a broken wing and luring away a dangerous animal.

Grey Plover
  de:Kiebitzregenpfeifer
  fr: Pluvier argenté
  es: Chorlito Gris
  ja: ダイゼン
  cn:灰鸻
Pluvialis squatarola

breeding

breeding

Photo O.W.Johnson

PD

Pacific Golden Plover
  de:Pazifischer Goldregenpfeifer
  fr: Pluvier fauve
  es:Chorlito Dorado Siberiano
  ja: アジアムナグロ
  cn:金鸻
Pluvialis fulva

breeding

Photo W.J.Daunicht

AU

Northern Lapwing
  de:Kiebitz
  fr: Vanneau huppé
  es:Avefría Europea
  ja: タゲリ
  cn:凤头麦鸡
Vanellus vanellus
Near threatened.

www.avitopia.net/bird.en/?vid=1325301
www.avitopia.net/bird.en/?aud=1325301

Photo J.M.Garg

S3.0

River Lapwing
  de:Flusskiebitz
  fr: Vanneau pie
  es:Avefría Fluvial
  ja: カタグロツバメゲリ
  cn:距翅麦鸡
Vanellus duvaucelii
Near threatened.

adult

Photo Pete Morris

S4.0

Grey-headed Lapwing
  de:Graukopfkiebitz
  fr: Vanneau à tête grise
  es:Avefría Ceniza
  ja: ケリ
  cn:灰头麦鸡
Vanellus cinereus

adult

Red-wattled Lapwing
  de:Rotlappenkiebitz
  fr: Vanneau indien
  es: Avefría India
  ja: インドトサカゲリ
  cn:肉垂麦鸡
Vanellus indicus

adult

Lesser Sand Plover
  de:Mongolenregenpfeifer
  fr: Pluvier de Mongolie
  es: Chorlitejo Mongol Chico
  ja: メダイチドリ
  cn:蒙古沙鸻
Charadrius mongolus

non-breeding

Greater Sand Plover
  de:Wüstenregenpfeifer
  fr: Pluvier de Leschenault
  es: Chorlitejo Mongol Grande
  ja: オオメダイチドリ
  cn:铁嘴沙鸻
Charadrius leschenaultii

non-breeding

Malaysian Plover
  de:Malaienregenpfeifer
  fr: Pluvier de Péron
  es: Chorlitejo Malayo
  ja: クロエリシロチドリ
  cn:马来鸻
Charadrius peronii
Near threatened.

♂ adult

AU

Photo W.J.Daunicht

♂ non-breeding

Kentish Plover
de:Seeregenpfeifer
fr: Pluvier à collier interrompu
es:Chorlitejo Patinegro
ja:シロチドリ
cn:环颈鸻
Charadrius alexandrinus

www.avitopia.net/bird.en/?vid=1325412

LIC

Photo W.D.G.Daunicht

♂ breeding

Common Ringed Plover
de:Sandregenpfeifer
fr: Pluvier grand-gravelot
es:Chorlitejo Grande
ja:ハジロコチドリ
cn:剑鸻
Charadrius hiaticula

www.avitopia.net/bird.en/?vid=1325416

S3.0

Photo M.Nishimura

adult

Long-billed Plover
de:Ussuriregenpfeifer
fr: Pluvier à long bec
es:Chorlitejo Piquilargo
ja:イカルチドリ
cn:长嘴剑鸻
Charadrius placidus

AU

Photo W.J.Daunicht

breeding

Little Ringed Plover
de:Flussregenpfeifer
fr: Pluvier petit-gravelot
es:Chorlitejo Chico
ja:コチドリ
cn:金眶鸻
Charadrius dubius

www.avitopia.net/bird.en/?vid=1325421

Oriental Plover
 de:Steppenregenpfeifer
 fr: Pluvier oriental
 es: Chorlito Asiático Grande
 ja: オオチドリ
 cn:东方鸻
Charadrius veredus

breeding

Painted Snipes - *Rostratulidae*

The family of Painted Snipes occurs in Africa, Eurasia, Australia and southern South America. The body length is 19 cm to 24 cm. They have wide wings and long legs with long toes. The females are larger than the males and have more contrasting patterns. As bad flyers, they are secretive, solitary ground birds that are active at dawn and dusk. They live on both small animals and seeds. The precocial chicks are looked after by the male.

Greater Painted Snipe
 de:Goldschnepfe
 fr: Rhynchée peinte
 es: Aguatero Bengalí
 ja: タマシギ
 cn:彩鹬
Rostratula benghalensis

♀ adult

Jacanas - *Jacanidae*

The family of Jacanas occurs from Africa through South Asia to Australia and in Central and South America. They become 15 cm to 50 cm long. Legs, toes and claws are long, the tail is usually short. Noteworthy is a thorn on the leading edge of the wing. Their habitat are the banks of lakes and swamps. They are very adept at walking over floating vegetation such as Water lily leaves. They eat small aquatic animals, but also seeds from aquatic plants. In most species, the males take care of the offspring.

S3.0

Photo Alnus

breeding

Pheasant-tailed Jacana
de:Wasserfasan
fr: Jacana à longue queue
es: Jacana Colilarga
ja: レンカク
cn:水雉
Hydrophasianus chirurgus

S3.0

Photo Kousik Nandy

adult

Bronze-winged Jacana
de:Hindublatthühnchen
fr: Jacana bronzé
es: Jacana Bronceada
ja: アジアレンカク
cn:铜翅水雉
Metopidius indicus

Sandpipers and Snipes - *Scolopacidae*

The family of Snipes is distributed worldwide, most of the species are migratory birds that sometimes cover great distances. The body length ranges from 13 cm to 60 cm. They usually live near water and outside the breeding season often form large flocks on the seashore. The diet consists of small invertebrates. The young birds leave the nest immediately after hatching.

Whimbrel
  de:Regenbrachvogel
  fr: Courlis corlieu
  es:Zarapito Trinador
  ja: チュウシャクシギ
  cn:中杓鷸
Numenius phaeopus

www.avitopia.net/bird.en/?vid=1450202

adult

Little Curlew
  de:Zwergbrachvogel
  fr: Courlis nain
  es:Zarapito Chico
  ja: コシャクシギ
  cn:小杓鷸
Numenius minutus

adult

Eastern Curlew
  de:Isabellbrachvogel
  fr: Courlis de Sibérie
  es:Zarapito Siberiano
  ja: ホウロクシギ
  cn:大杓鷸
Numenius madagascariensis
Endangered.

adult

AU

adult

Eurasian Curlew
  de: Großer Brachvogel
  fr: Courlis cendré
  es: Zarapito Real
  ja: ダイシャクシギ
  cn: 白腰杓鷸
Numenius arquata
Near threatened.

Photo W.J.Daunicht

www.avitopia.net/bird.en/?vid=1450208
www.avitopia.net/bird.en/?aud=1450208

PD

breeding

Bar-tailed Godwit
  de: Pfuhlschnepfe
  fr: Barge rousse
  es: Aguja Colipinta
  ja: オオソリハシシギ
  cn: 斑尾塍鷸
Limosa lapponica
Near threatened.

Photo S.Maslowski

www.avitopia.net/bird.en/?vid=1450301

AU

breeding

Black-tailed Godwit
  de: Uferschnepfe
  fr: Barge à queue noire
  es: Aguja Colinegra
  ja: オグロシギ
  cn: 黑尾塍鷸
Limosa limosa
Near threatened.

Photo W.J.Daunicht

www.avitopia.net/bird.en/?vid=1450302
www.avitopia.net/bird.en/?aud=1450302

PD

breeding

Ruddy Turnstone
  de: Steinwälzer
  fr: Tournepierre à collier
  es: Vuelvepiedras Común
  ja: キョウジョシギ
  cn: 翻石鷸
Arenaria interpres

Photo T.Bowman

61

Great Knot
de:Großer Knutt
fr: Bécasseau de l'Anadyr
es:Correlimos Grande
ja:オバシギ
cn:大滨鹬
Calidris tenuirostris
Endangered.

breeding

Red Knot
de:Knutt
fr: Bécasseau maubèche
es:Correlimos Gordo
ja:コオバシギ
cn:红腹滨鹬
Calidris canutus
Near threatened.

breeding

Ruff
de:Kampfläufer
fr: Combattant varié
es:Combatiente
ja:エリマキシギ
cn:流苏鹬
Calidris pugnax

www.avitopia.net/bird.en/?vid=1450604
www.avitopia.net/bird.en/?wid=1450604

♂ breeding

Broad-billed Sandpiper
de:Sumpfläufer
fr: Bécasseau falcinelle
es:Correlimos Falcinelo
ja:キリアイ
cn:阔嘴鹬
Calidris falcinellus

adult

breeding

Photo L.Karney

PD

Sharp-tailed Sandpiper
de:Spitzschwanz-Strandläufer
fr: Bécasseau à queue pointue
es:Correlimos Acuminado
ja: ウズラシギ
cn:尖尾滨鹬
Calidris acuminata

breeding

Photo Davidvraju

S4.0

Curlew Sandpiper
de:Sichelstrandläufer
fr: Bécasseau cocorli
es:Correlimos Zarapitín
ja: サルハマシギ
cn:弯嘴滨鹬
Calidris ferruginea
Near threatened.

breeding

Photo Andreas Trepte

S2.5

Temminck's Stint
de:Temminckstrandläufer
fr: Bécasseau de Temminck
es:Correlimos de Temminck
ja: オジロトウネン
cn:青脚滨鹬
Calidris temminckii

breeding

Drawing H.Groenvold

PD

Long-toed Stint
de:Langzehen-Strandläufer
fr: Bécasseau à longs doigts
es:Correlimos Dedilargo
ja: ヒバリシギ
cn:长趾滨鹬
Calidris subminuta

Spoon-billed Sandpiper
 de:Löffelstrandläufer
 fr: Bécasseau spatule
 es:Correlimos Cuchareta
 ja:ヘラシギ
 cn:勺嘴鹬
Calidris pygmea
Critically endangered.

breeding

Red-necked Stint
 de:Rotkehl-Strandläufer
 fr: Bécasseau à col roux
 es:Correlimos Cuellirrojo
 ja:トウネン
 cn:红颈滨鹬
Calidris ruficollis
Near threatened.

breeding

Sanderling
 de:Sanderling
 fr: Bécasseau sanderling
 es:Correlimos Tridáctilo
 ja:ミユビシギ
 cn:三趾滨鹬
Calidris alba

non-breeding

Dunlin
 de:Alpenstrandläufer
 fr: Bécasseau variable
 es:Correlimos Común
 ja:ハマシギ
 cn:黑腹滨鹬
Calidris alpina

www.avitopia.net/bird.en/?vid=1450614

breeding

LIC

Photo W.D.G.Daunicht

breeding

Pectoral Sandpiper
  de: Graubrust-Strandläufer
  fr: Bécasseau à poitrine cendrée
  es: Correlimos Pectoral
  ja: アメリカウズラシギ
  cn: 斑胸滨鹬
Calidris melanotos

S4.0

Photo Ray Tipper

adult

Asian Dowitcher
  de: Steppenschlammläufer
  fr: Bécassin d'Asie
  es: Agujeta Asiática
  ja: シベリアオオハシシギ
  cn: 半蹼鹬
Limnodromus semipalmatus
Near threatened.

S3.0

Photo Durzan Cirano

adult

Jack Snipe
  de: Zwergschnepfe
  fr: Bécassine sourde
  es: Agachadiza Chica
  ja: コシギ
  cn: 姬鹬
Lymnocryptes minimus

A2.0

Photo Jason Thompson

adult

Eurasian Woodcock
  de: Waldschnepfe
  fr: Bécasse des bois
  es: Chocha Perdiz
  ja: ヤマシギ
  cn: 丘鹬
Scolopax rusticola

Wood Snipe
  de:Nepalbekassine
  fr: Bécassine des bois
  es: Agachadiza del Himalaya
  ja: モリジシギ
  cn:林沙锥
Gallinago nemoricola
Vulnerable.

adult

Common Snipe
  de:Bekassine
  fr: Bécassine des marais
  es: Agachadiza común
  ja: タシギ
  cn:扇尾沙锥
Gallinago gallinago

adult

Pin-tailed Snipe
  de:Spießbekassine
  fr: Bécassine à queue pointue
  es: Agachadiza Colirrara
  ja: ハリオシギ
  cn:针尾沙锥
Gallinago stenura

adult

Swinhoe's Snipe
  de:Waldbekassine
  fr: Bécassine de Swinhoe
  es: Agachadiza del Baikal
  ja: チュウジシギ
  cn:大沙锥
Gallinago megala

adult

adult

Photo Alpsdake

S3.0

Terek Sandpiper
de:Terekwasserläufer
fr: Chevalier bargette
es: Andarríos del Terek
ja: ソリハシシギ
cn:翘嘴鹬
Xenus cinereus

♀ breeding

Photo W.J.Daunicht

AU

Red-necked Phalarope
de:Odinshühnchen
fr: Phalarope à bec étroit
es: Falaropo Picofino
ja: アカエリヒレアシシギ
cn:红颈瓣蹼鹬
Phalaropus lobatus

adult

Photo W.J.Daunicht

AU

Common Sandpiper
de:Flussuferläufer
fr: Chevalier guignette
es: Andarríos Chico
ja: イソシギ
cn:矶鹬
Actitis hypoleucos

 www.avitopia.net/bird.en/?vid=1451401

adult

Photo W.J.Daunicht

AU

Green Sandpiper
de:Waldwasserläufer
fr: Chevalier cul-blanc
es: Andarríos Grande
ja: クサシギ
cn:白腰草鹬
Tringa ochropus

 www.avitopia.net/bird.en/?vid=1451501

Grey-tailed Tattler
de:Grauschwanz-Wasserläufer
fr: Chevalier de Sibérie
es:Playero Siberiano
ja:キアシシギ
cn:灰尾漂鷸
Tringa brevipes
Near threatened.

breeding

Spotted Redshank
de:Dunkler Wasserläufer
fr: Chevalier arlequin
es: Archibebe Oscuro
ja:ツルシギ
cn:鶴鷸
Tringa erythropus

breeding

Common Greenshank
de:Grünschenkel
fr: Chevalier aboyeur
es: Archibebe Claro
ja:アオアシシギ
cn:青脚鷸
Tringa nebularia

breeding

Nordmann's Greenshank
de:Tüpfelgrünschenkel
fr: Chevalier tacheté
es: Archibebe Moteado
ja:カラフトアオアシシギ
cn:小青脚鷸
Tringa guttifer
Endangered.

non-breeding

breeding

Photo Alnus

S3.0

Marsh Sandpiper
de: Teichwasserläufer
fr: Chevalier stagnatile
es: Archibebe Fino
ja: コアオアシシギ
cn: 泽鹬
Tringa stagnatilis

adult

Photo W.J.Daunicht

AU

Wood Sandpiper
de: Bruchwasserläufer
fr: Chevalier sylvain
es: Andarríos Bastardo
ja: タカブシギ
cn: 林鹬
Tringa glareola

 www.avitopia.net/bird.en/?vid=1451512

breeding

Photo W.J.Daunicht

AU

Common Redshank
de: Rotschenkel
fr: Chevalier gambette
es: Archibebe Común
ja: アカアシシギ
cn: 红脚鹬
Tringa totanus

www.avitopia.net/bird.en/?vid=1451513
www.avitopia.net/bird.en/?aud=1451513

Button-quails - *Turnicidae*

The family of Button-quails is common in Africa, Eurasia, Australia, and even some islands in the Pacific. They are small birds, only 11 cm to 19 cm long. The wings are short and rounded, the tail is very short. The short, strong legs have 3 toes. They live on the ground, are shy and rarely fly. During courtship, the female dominates, the males breed and later care for the precocial chicks.

Small Buttonquail
  de: Laufhühnchen
  fr: Turnix d'Andalousie
  es: Torillo Andaluz
  ja: ヒメミフウズラ
  cn: 林三趾鹑
Turnix sylvaticus

adult

Yellow-legged Buttonquail
  de: Rotnacken-Laufhühnchen
  fr: Turnix indien
  es: Torillo Tanki
  ja: チョウセンミフウズラ
  cn: 黄脚三趾鹑
Turnix tanki

♀ adult

Barred Buttonquail
  de: Bindenlaufhühnchen
  fr: Turnix combattant
  es: Torillo Batallador
  ja: ミフウズラ
  cn: 棕三趾鹑
Turnix suscitator

www.avitopia.net/bird.en/?vid=1475106

adult

Coursers and Pratincoles - *Glareolidae*

The family of Coursers and Pratincoles is common in the Old World. They are 15 cm to 25 cm long. The Coursers have long legs, short wide wings and a longer beak, while the Pratincoles have long pointed wings, a forked tail, medium-long legs and a short beak. Coursers are ground birds and good runners, Pratincoles are good fliers whose flight style is reminiscent of swallows. The nest is dug out on the ground; both parents breed and take care of the precocial chicks.

$2.0

Photo Charles Lam

adult

Oriental Pratincole
  de: Orientbrachschwalbe
  fr: Glaréole orientale
  es: Canastera Oriental
  ja: ツバメチドリ
  cn: 普通燕鸻
Glareola maldivarum

$3.0

Photo Kousik Nandy&Sumana Paul

adult

Small Pratincole
  de: Sandbrachschwalbe
  fr: Glaréole lactée
  es: Canastera Chica
  ja: ヒメツバメチドリ
  cn: 灰燕鸻
Glareola lactea

Jaegers - *Stercorariidae*

The family of Jaegers is native to the arctic and subarctic areas of the northern and southern hemispheres. They migrate very far and can spend indefinite time at sea. The body length ranges from 40 cm to 60 cm. Their feet are webbed and have strong claws. The beak is strong and has a curved tip. Skuas are very fast and agile fliers. They breed near bird colonies and are aggressive predators and parasites there. They chase other birds until they vomit their food.

Pomarine Jaeger
  de:Spatelraubmöwe
  fr: Labbe pomarin
  es:Págalo Pomarino
  ja: トウゾクカモメ
  cn:中贼鸥
Stercorarius pomarinus

adult

Parasitic Jaeger
  de:Schmarotzerraubmöwe
  fr: Labbe parasite
  es:Págalo Parásito
  ja: クロトウゾクカモメ
  cn:短尾贼鸥
Stercorarius parasiticus

adult, dark phase

Long-tailed Jaeger
  de:Falkenraubmöwe
  fr: Labbe à longue queue
  es:Págalo Rabero
  ja: シロハラトウゾクカモメ
  cn:长尾贼鸥
Stercorarius longicaudus

adult

Gulls - *Laridae*

The family of Gulls is found worldwide, most of the species are migratory birds. The body length ranges from 20 cm to 75 cm. Gulls are strongly built, they have long, pointed wings and a rather long tail. Their feet are webbed. They are very good fliers who often sail or glide. They can also swim well, but few species dive. They often breed in large colonies.

adult

Photo John Holmes

S4.0

Saunders's Gull
  de:Saundersmöwe
  fr: Mouette de Saunders
  es: Gaviota de Saunders
  ja: ズグロカモメ
  cn:黑嘴鸥
Saundersilarus saundersi
Vulnerable.

breeding

Photo W.J.Daunicht

AU

Common Black-headed Gull
  de:Lachmöwe
  fr: Mouette rieuse
  es: Gaviota Reidora
  ja: ユリカモメ
  cn:红嘴鸥
Chroicocephalus ridibundus

🔊 www.avitopia.net/bird.en/?kom=1600610
  www.avitopia.net/bird.en/?vid=1600610
  www.avitopia.net/bird.en/?wid=1600610

breeding

Drawing J.G.Keulemans

PD

Brown-headed Gull
  de:Braunkopfmöwe
  fr: Mouette du Tibet
  es: Gaviota Centroasiática
  ja: チャガシラカモメ
  cn:棕头鸥
Chroicocephalus brunnicephalus

Relict Gull
de: Reliktmöwe
fr: Mouette relique
es: Gaviota Relicta
ja: ゴビズキンカモメ
cn: 遗鸥
Ichthyaetus relictus
Vulnerable.

♂♀ breeding

Mew Gull
de: Sturmmöwe
fr: Goéland cendré
es: Gaviota Cana
ja: カモメ
cn: 海鸥
Larus canus

www.avitopia.net/bird.en/?vid=1601106

breeding

Herring Gull
de: Silbermöwe
fr: Goéland argenté
es: Gaviota Argéntea
ja: セグロカモメ
cn: 银鸥
Larus argentatus

www.avitopia.net/bird.en/?vid=1601111

breeding

Brown Noddy
de: Noddi
fr: Noddi brun
es: Tiñosa Boba
ja: クロアジサシ
cn: 白顶玄燕鸥
Anous stolidus

adult

adult

A2.0

Sooty Tern
de:Rußseeschwalbe
fr: Sterne fuligineuse
es:Charrán Sombrío
ja:セグロアジサシ
cn:乌燕鸥
Onychoprion fuscatus

Photo Drew Avery

adult

PD

Bridled Tern
de:Zügelseeschwalbe
fr: Sterne bridée
es:Charrán Embridado
ja:マミジロアジサシ
cn:褐翅燕鸥
Onychoprion anaethetus

Drawing A.Thorburn

breeding

A2.0

Little Tern
de:Zwergseeschwalbe
fr: Sterne naine
es:Charrancito Común
ja:コアジサシ
cn:白额燕鸥
Sternula albifrons

Photo Agustin Povedano

adult

S2.0

Gull-billed Tern
de:Lachseeschwalbe
fr: Sterne hansel
es:Pagaza Piconegra
ja:ハシブトアジサシ
cn:鸥嘴噪鸥
Gelochelidon nilotica

Photo Charles Lam

Caspian Tern
de:Raubseeschwalbe
fr: Sterne caspienne
es: Pagaza Piquirroja
ja: オニアジサシ
cn:红嘴巨鸥
Hydroprogne caspia

breeding

White-winged Tern
de:Weißflügel-Seeschwalbe
fr: Guifette leucoptère
es: Fumarel Aliblanco
ja: ハジロクロハラアジサシ
cn:白翅浮鸥
Chlidonias leucopterus

breeding

Whiskered Tern
de:Weißbart-Seeschwalbe
fr: Guifette moustac
es: Fumarel cariblanco
ja: クロハラアジサシ
cn:须浮鸥
Chlidonias hybrida

breeding

Roseate Tern
de:Rosenseeschwalbe
fr: Sterne de Dougall
es: Charrán Rosado
ja: ベニアジサシ
cn:粉红燕鸥
Sterna dougallii

breeding

adult

Drawing J.G.Keulemans

Black-naped Tern
de:Schwarznacken-Seeschwalbe
fr: Sterne diamant
es:Charrán de Sumatra
ja: エリグロアジサシ
cn:黒枕燕鴎
Sterna sumatrana

♂ breeding

Photo W.J.Daunicht

Common Tern
de:Flussseeschwalbe
fr: Sterne pierregarin
es:Charrán Común
ja: アジサシ
cn:普通燕鴎
Sterna hirundo

breeding

Photo D.Dewhurst

Arctic Tern
de:Küstenseeschwalbe
fr: Sterne arctique
es:Charrán Artico
ja: キョクアジサシ
cn:北极燕鴎
Sterna paradisaea

adult

Drawing Pretre

Black-bellied Tern
de:Schwarzbauch-Seeschwalbe
fr: Sterne à ventre noir
es:Charrán Ventrinegro
ja: インドアジサシ
cn:黑腹燕鴎
Sterna acuticauda
Endangered.

River Tern
 de:Hinduseeschwalbe
 fr: Sterne de rivière
 es: Charrán Indio
 ja: カワアジサシ
 cn:黄嘴河燕鸥
Sterna aurantia
Near threatened.

breeding

Swift Tern
 de:Eilseeschwalbe
 fr: Sterne huppée
 es: Charrán Piquigualdo
 ja: オオアジサシ
 cn:大凤头燕鸥
Thalasseus bergii

breeding

Lesser Crested Tern
 de:Rüppellseeschwalbe
 fr: Sterne voyageuse
 es: Charrán Bengalí
 ja: ベンガルアジサシ
 cn:小凤头燕鸥
Thalasseus bengalensis

adult

Indian Skimmer
 de:Indischer Scherenschnabel
 fr: Bec-en-ciseaux à collier
 es: Rayador Indio
 ja: シロエリハサミアジサシ
 cn:剪嘴鸥
Rynchops albicollis
Vulnerable.

adult

Pigeons and Doves - *Columbidae*

The family of Pigeons and Doves is found all over the world except in the coldest regions. The body lengths range from 15 cm to 84 cm. They have medium-sized wings and often a long tail. The beak is rather short and not strong. The sexes are mostly the same. Their diet is predominantly vegetarian. The naked young birds are fed 'pigeon milk', a secretion that is formed in the parents' goiter.

Photo W.J.Daunicht

adult

AU Common Pigeon
de:Felsentaube
fr: Pigeon biset
es:Paloma Bravía
ja:カワラバト(ドバト)
cn:原鸽
Columba livia
Introduced.

🎞 www.avitopia.net/bird.en/?vid=1650101
🔊 www.avitopia.net/bird.en/?aud=1650101

Drawing G.E.Lodge

adult

PD Ashy Wood Pigeon
de:Himalayataube
fr: Pigeon cendré
es:Paloma Cenicienta
ja:タイワンジュズカケバト
cn:灰林鸽
Columba pulchricollis

Drawing H.Groenvold

♂♀ adult

PD Pale-capped Pigeon
de:Kupfertaube
fr: Pigeon marron
es:Paloma Purpúrea
ja:ムラサキモリバト
cn:紫林鸽
Columba punicea
Vulnerable.

Oriental Turtle Dove
 de:Orientturteltaube
 fr: Tourterelle orientale
 es: Tórtola Oriental
 ja: キジバト
 cn:山斑鸠
Streptopelia orientalis

adult

Eurasian Collared Dove
 de:Türkentaube
 fr: Tourterelle turque
 es: Tórtola Turca
 ja: シラコバト
 cn:灰斑鸠
Streptopelia decaocto

 www.avitopia.net/bird.en/?kom=1650507
www.avitopia.net/bird.en/?vid=1650507

adult

Red Turtle Dove
 de:Zwerglachtaube
 fr: Tourterelle à tête grise
 es: Tórtola Cabecigrís
 ja: ベニバト
 cn:火斑鸠
Streptopelia tranquebarica

adult

Spotted Dove
 de:Perlhalstaube
 fr: Tourterelle tigrine
 es: Tórtola Moteada
 ja: カノコバト
 cn:珠颈斑鸠
Streptopelia chinensis

♂♀ adult

♂ adult

PD **Barred Cuckoo-Dove**
　de:Bindenschwanztaube
　fr: Phasianelle onchall
　es: Tórtola-cuco Unchal
　ja: ヨコジマオナガバト
　cn:斑尾鹃鸠
Macropygia unchall

www.avitopia.net/bird.en/?vid=1650601

♂ adult

PD **Little Cuckoo-Dove**
　de:Rotmanteltaube
　fr: Phasianelle à tête rousse
　es: Tórtola-cuco Chica
　ja: ヒメオナガバト
　cn:小赤鹃鸠
Macropygia ruficeps

adult

AU **Common Emerald Dove**
　de:Graukappen-Glanztaube
　fr: Colombine turvert
　es: Palomita Esmeralda Dorsiverde
　ja: キンバト
　cn:绿翅金鸠
Chalcophaps indica

www.avitopia.net/bird.en/?vid=1651101

adult

AU **Zebra Dove**
　de:Sperbertäubchen
　fr: Géopélie zébrée
　es: Tortolita Estriada
　ja: チョウショウバト
　cn:斑姬地鸠
Geopelia striata

Pink-necked Green Pigeon
de:Frühlingstaube
fr: Colombar giouanne
es: Vinago Cuellirrosa
ja: コアオバト
cn:红颈绿鸠
Treron vernans

♂ adult

Orange-breasted Green Pigeon
de:Bindengrüntaube
fr: Colombar à double collier
es: Vinago Bicinta
ja: ムネアカアオバト
cn:橙胸绿鸠
Treron bicinctus

♂♀ adult

Ashy-headed Green-Pigeon
de:Aschkopf-Pompadourtaube
fr: Colombar de Phayre
es: Vinago del Himalaya
ja: ハイガシラアオバト
cn:*灰头绿鸠
Treron phayrei
Near threatened.

♂ adult

Thick-billed Green Pigeon
de:Papageischnabeltaube
fr: Colombar à gros bec
es: Vinago Piquigrueso
ja: ハシブトアオバト
cn:厚嘴绿鸠
Treron curvirostra

adult

♂ adult

S2.0 **Yellow-footed Green Pigeon**
de:Rotschultertaube
fr: Colombar commandeur
es: Vinago Patigualdo
ja: キアシアオバト
cn:黄脚绿鸠
Treron phoenicopterus

Photo Lip Kee Yap

adult

S4.0 **Yellow-vented Green Pigeon**
de:Weißbauch-Grüntaube
fr: Colombar de Seimund
es: Vinago Culigualdo
ja: シロハラハリオアオバト
cn:白腹针尾绿鸠
Treron seimundi

Photo Yaitz331

adult

PD **Pin-tailed Green Pigeon**
de:Spitzschwanz-Grüntaube
fr: Colombar à longue queue
es: Vinago Rabudo
ja: ハリオアオバト
cn:针尾绿鸠
Treron apicauda

Drawing H.Groenvold

adult

PD **Wedge-tailed Green Pigeon**
de:Keilschwanz-Grüntaube
fr: Colombar chanteur
es: Vinago Rabocuña
ja: オナガアオバト
cn:楔尾绿鸠
Treron sphenurus

Drawing P.L.Oudart

White-bellied Green Pigeon

de:Sieboldgrüntaube
fr: Colombar de Siebold
es: Vinago Japonés
ja: アオバト
cn:红翅绿鸠

Treron sieboldii

PD

Drawing Pretre

♂ adult

Green Imperial Pigeon

de:Bronzefruchttaube
fr: Carpophage pauline
es: Dúcula Verde
ja: ミカドバト
cn:绿皇鸠

Ducula aenea

www.avitopia.net/bird.en/?vid=1654406

AU

Photo W.J.Daunicht

adult

Mountain Imperial Pigeon

de:Fahlbauch-Fruchttaube
fr: Carpophage à manteau brun
es: Dúcula Dorsicastaña
ja: ヤマミカドバト
cn:皇鸠

Ducula badia

PD

Drawing G.E.Lodge

adult

Pied Imperial Pigeon

de:Zweifarben-Fruchttaube
fr: Carpophage blanc
es: Dúcula Bicolor
ja: ソデグロバト
cn:斑皇鸠

Ducula bicolor

www.avitopia.net/bird.en/?vid=1654436

AU

Photo W.J.Daunicht

adult

Cuckoos - *Cuculidae*

The family of Cuckoos is found worldwide except in the coldest areas. Many species are migratory birds. Cuckoos often have slender bodies and very long tails. The body length ranges from 17 cm to 70 cm. Except for the Roadrunners, the legs are short, with two toes pointing forward and two pointing backwards. The sexes are mostly the same. They feed mainly on insects. Many species are pronounced brood parasites. After hatching, the young cuckoos regularly push the other nest siblings out of the nest. The non-parasitic species are able to build nests. With the exception of the Anis, cuckoos are loners.

Photo Alois Staudacher · S3.0

adult

Coral-billed Ground Cuckoo
de: Renauldkuckuck
fr: Calobate de l'Annam
es: Cuco Terrestre de Indochina
ja: アカハシハシリカッコウ
cn: 瑞氏红嘴地鹃
Carpococcyx renauldi

Photo W.J.Daunicht · AU

adult

Greater Coucal
de: Heckenkuckuck
fr: Grand Coucal
es: Cucal Chino
ja: オオバンケンバンケン
cn: 褐翅鸦鹃
Centropus sinensis

Drawing E.Travies · PD

adult

Lesser Coucal
de: Bengalenkuckuck
fr: Coucal rufin
es: Cucal Bengalí
ja: バンケン
cn: 小鸦鹃
Centropus bengalensis

Green-billed Malkoha
 de: Großer Grünschnabelkuckuck
 fr: Malcoha sombre
 es: Malcoha Sombrío
 ja: オニクロバンケンモドキ
 cn: 大绿嘴地鹃
Phaenicophaeus tristis

adult

Chestnut-winged Cuckoo
 de: Koromandelkuckuck
 fr: Coucou à collier
 es: Críalo Oriental
 ja: カンムリカッコウ
 cn: 红翅凤头鹃
Clamator coromandus

adult

Asian Koel
 de: Indischer Koel
 fr: Coucou koël
 es: Koel Común
 ja: オニカッコウ
 cn: 噪鹃
Eudynamys scolopaceus

♂ adult

Asian Emerald Cuckoo
 de: Prachtkuckuck
 fr: Coucou émeraude
 es: Cuclillo Esmeralda Asiático
 ja: ミドリテリカッコウ
 cn: 翠金鹃
Chrysococcyx maculatus

♂ adult

Drawing J.Gould&W.M.Hart

PD

Violet Cuckoo
de:Amethystkuckuck
fr: Coucou violet
es: Cuclillo Violeta
ja: スミレテリカッコウ
cn:紫金鹃
Chrysococcyx xanthorhynchus

adult

Photo Sandeep Gangadharan

A2.0

Banded Bay Cuckoo
de:Sonneratkuckuck
fr: Coucou de Sonnerat
es: Cuco Bayo
ja: クリイロヒメカッコウ
cn:栗斑杜鹃
Cacomantis sonneratii

adult

Drawing G.A.Levett-Yeats

PD

Plaintive Cuckoo
de:Klagekuckuck
fr: Coucou plaintif
es: Cuco Plañidero
ja: ヒメカッコウ
cn:八声杜鹃
Cacomantis merulinus

adult

Photo Eric Gropp

A2.0

Asian Drongo-Cuckoo
de:Drongokuckuck
fr: Coucou surnicou
es: Cuclillo-drongo Asiático
ja: オウチュウカッコウ
cn:乌鹃
Surniculus lugubris

adult

Large Hawk-Cuckoo
  de:Großer Sperberkuckuck
  fr: Coucou épervier
  es: Cuco Grande
  ja: オオジュウイチ
  cn:鹰鹃
Hierococcyx sparverioides

adult

Rufous Hawk-Cuckoo
  de:Nördlicher Fluchtkuckuck
  fr: Coucou de Chine
  es: Cuco Fujitivo Norteño
  ja: キタジュウイチ
  cn:北鹰鹃
Hierococcyx hyperythrus

adult

Hodgson's Hawk-Cuckoo
  de:Hodgsonkuckuck
  fr: Coucou de Hodgson
  es: Cuco de Hodgson
  ja: ジュウイチ
  cn:霍氏鹰鹃
Hierococcyx nisicolor

adult

Lesser Cuckoo
  de:Gackelkuckuck
  fr: Petit Coucou
  es: Cuco Chico
  ja: ホトトギス
  cn:小杜鹃
Cuculus poliocephalus

♀ adult

Photo Sandeep Gangadharan

A2.0

♂ juvenile

Indian Cuckoo
de:Kurzflügelkuckuck
fr: Coucou à ailes courtes
es:Cuco Alicorto
ja:セグロカッコウ
cn:四声杜鹃
Cuculus micropterus

Photo Ron Knight

A2.0

adult

Oriental Cuckoo
de:Himalaya-Hopfkuckuck
fr: Coucou de l'Himalaya
es:Cuco del Himalaya
ja:ツツドリ
cn:中杜鹃
Cuculus saturatus

Photo GabrielBuissart

S3.0

adult

Common Cuckoo
de:Kuckuck
fr: Coucou gris
es:Cuco Común
ja:カッコウ
cn:大杜鹃
Cuculus canorus

 www.avitopia.net/bird.en/?kom=1728210
www.avitopia.net/bird.en/?aud=1728210

Photo Aviceda

S3.0

adult

Northern Oriental Cuckoo
de:Orient-Hopfkuckuck
fr: Coucou oriental
es:Cuco oriental
ja:ツツドリ
cn:霍氏中杜鹃
Cuculus optatus

Barn owls - *Tytonidae*

The family of Barn Owls includes only a few species, but one of them is a true cosmopolitan. It occurs on all continents and only avoids the colder areas of the earth. The body length ranges from 23 cm to 55 cm. The legs are quite long, the central claw is comb-like. The head is endowed with a conspicuous veil and has a curved beak. Barn owls are nocturnal hunters that fly noiselessly near the ground. They can hear directionally and are able to locate their prey by hearing only.

Eastern Grass-Owl
  de:Graseule
  fr: Effraie de prairie
  es: Lechuza Patilarga
  ja: ヒガシメンフクロウ
  cn:草鸮
Tyto longimembris

adult, juvenile

Barn Owl
  de:Schleiereule
  fr: Effraie des clochers
  es: Lechuza Común
  ja: メンフクロウ
  cn:仓鸮
Tyto alba

www.avitopia.net/bird.en/?vid=1750112

adult

Oriental Bay Owl
  de:Maskeneule
  fr: Phodile calong
  es: Lechuza Cornuda
  ja: コンゴニセメンフクロウ
  cn:栗鸮
Phodilus badius

adult

Drawing J.Gould&H.C.Richter

Photo W.J.Daunicht

Photo W.J.Daunicht

Owls - *Strigidae*

The family of Owls is found worldwide. They have compact bodies (13 cm - 70 cm) and usually wide wings and rounded tails. The toes are strong, one of which is a turning toe that helps with grip. The head is large, the neck short. The eyes are directed rather forward, the beak is short and hook-shaped. Owls mainly hunt at night, benefiting from their noiseless flight and sharp hearing.

adult

Drawing J.G.Keulemans

PD Mountain Scops Owl
de:Fuchseule
fr: Petit-duc tacheté
es: Autillo Moteado
ja: タイワンコノハズク
cn:黄嘴角鸮
Otus spilocephalus
Near threatened.

adult

Drawing M.Arnoul

PD Collared Scops Owl
de:Halsband-Zwergohreule
fr: Petit-duc à collier
es: Autillo Chino
ja: ヒガシオオコノハズク
cn:领角鸮
Otus lettia

adult

Drawing J.G.Keulemans

PD Oriental Scops Owl
de:Orient-Zwergohreule
fr: Petit-duc d'Orient
es: Autillo Oriental
ja: コノハズク
cn:红角鸮
Otus sunia

Spot-bellied Eagle-Owl

de:Nepaluhu
fr: Grand-duc du Népal
es:Búho Nepalí
ja:ネパアルワシミミズク
cn:林雕鸮

Bubo nipalensis

adult

PD

Drawing J.G.Keulemans

Brown Fish Owl

de:Fischuhu
fr: Kétoupa brun
es:Búho Pescador de Ceilán
ja:ミナミシマフクロウ
cn:褐渔鸮

Ketupa zeylonensis

adult

S3.0

Photo Somaskanda

Tawny Fish Owl

de:Himalayafischuhu
fr: Kétoupa roux
es:Búho Pescador Leonado
ja:ウオミミズク
cn:黄腿渔鸮

Ketupa flavipes

adult

A3.0

Photo Jayanthsharma at en.wikipedia

Buffy Fish Owl

de:Sundafischuhu
fr: Kétoupa malais
es:Búho Pescador Malayo
ja:マレアウオミミズク
cn:马来渔鸮

Ketupa ketupu

www.avitopia.net/bird.en/?vid=1776104

adult

AU

Photo W.J.Daunicht

adult

PD **Collared Owlet**
 de: Wachtelkauz
 fr: Chevêchette à collier
 es: Mochuelo Acollarado
 ja: ヒメフクロウ
 cn: 领鸺鹠
Glaucidium brodiei

Drawing J.Gould&H.C.Richter

adult

PD **Asian Barred Owlet**
 de: Kuckuckstrillerkauz
 fr: Chevêchette cuculoïde
 es: Mochuelo Cuco
 ja: オオスズメフクロウ
 cn: 斑头鸺鹠
Glaucidium cuculoides

Drawing J.&E.Gould

adult

PD **Spotted Owlet**
 de: Brahmakauz
 fr: Chevêche brame
 es: Mochuelo Brahmán
 ja: インドコキンメフクロウ
 cn: 横斑腹小鸮
Athene brama

Drawing Pretre

adult

AU **Spotted Wood Owl**
 de: Pagodenkauz
 fr: Chouette des pagodes
 es: Cárabo de las Pagodas
 ja: マレアモリフクロウ
 cn: 点斑林鸮
Strix seloputo

Photo W.J.Daunicht

Brown Wood Owl
de:Malaienkauz
fr: Chouette leptogramme
es: Cárabo Oriental
ja: オオフクロウ
cn:褐林鸮
Strix leptogrammica

www.avitopia.net/bird.en/?vid=1776903

adult

Himalayan Owl
de:Himalajakauz
fr: Chouette de l'Himalaya
es: Cárabo del Himalaya
ja: ヒマラヤフクロウ
cn:灰林鸮
Strix nivicolum

adult

Long-eared Owl
de:Waldohreule
fr: Hibou moyen-duc
es: Búho Chico
ja: トラフズク
cn:长耳鸮
Asio otus

www.avitopia.net/bird.en/?vid=1777001

adult

Short-eared Owl
de:Sumpfohreule
fr: Hibou des marais
es: Búho Campestre
ja: コミミズク
cn:短耳鸮
Asio flammeus

adult

S3.0

Photo M.Nishimura

Brown Hawk-Owl
de:Falkenkauz
fr: Ninoxe hirsute
es:Lechuza Gavilana Castaña
ja: アオバズク
cn:鷹鴞
Ninox scutulata

adult

Frogmouths - *Podargidae*

The family of Frogmouths is widespread from India to Southeast Asia to Australia. They grow to be 20 cm to 53 cm lang. Their neck is short and as thick as their head. Characteristic is the wide and flat beak with a curved tip, the wide throat and the cryptic plumage. Their habitat are wooded landscapes. They feed on larger invertebrates such as millipedes, scorpions, and snails, but also eat small vertebrates and fruits. They are usually found in pairs and rest lengthways on a branch. One or two eggs are laid in their nest made of twigs, both parents incubate for about 30 days. Both also take care of the chicks until they fledge after about 30 days.

Drawing J.Wolf

PD

Hodgson's Frogmouth
de:Langschwanz-Froschmaul
fr: Podarge de Hodgson
es:Podargo Colilargo
ja: メスボシガマグチヨタカ
cn:黑顶蟆口鸱
Batrachostomus hodgsoni

adult

Drawing J.Smit

PD

Blyth's Frogmouth
de:Malaienfroschmaul
fr: Podarge de Blyth
es:Podargo de Blyth
ja: コガマグチヨタカ
cn:星喉蟆口鸱
Batrachostomus affinis

♀ adult

Nightjars - *Caprimulgidae*

The family of Nightjars is found all over the world, with the exception of the colder areas and New Zealand. The body length is between 19 cm and 30 cm, but elongated wing feathers appear in two species. Nightjars have long wings and tails, but their legs, toes, and claws are small. The beak is also small, but the throat is very wide. They are crepuscular and nocturnal and sit motionless on the ground or on a branch during the day. They feed on insects that they prey on in flight. The eggs are usually laid directly on the ground. There are also species among the nightjars that hibernate.

Great Eared Nightjar
  de:Riesennachtschwalbe
  fr: Engoulevent oreillard
  es:Chotacabras Orejudo
  ja:オオミミヨタカ
  cn:毛腿夜鷹
Lyncornis macrotis

♂ adult

Drawing J.G.Keulemans

Gray Nightjar
  de:Graunachtschwalbe
  fr: Engoulevent jotaka
  es:Chotacabras Jotaka
  ja:ヨタカ
  cn:*普通夜鷹
Caprimulgus jotaka

♂ adult

Drawing J.Wolf

Large-tailed Nightjar
  de:Langschwanz-Nachtschwalbe
  fr: Engoulevent de Horsfield
  es:Chotacabras Macruro
  ja:オビロヨタカ
  cn:长尾夜鷹
Caprimulgus macrurus

adult

Drawing R.Green

adult, pullus

A2.0
Indian Nightjar
  de:Hindunachtschwalbe
  fr: Engoulevent indien
  es:Chotacabras Hindú
  ja:インドヨタカ
  cn:印度夜鹰
Caprimulgus asiaticus

Photo Brian Gratwicke

♂ adult

PD
Savanna Nightjar
  de:Savannennachtschwalbe
  fr: Engoulevent affin
  es:Chotacabras de Sabana
  ja:シロアゴヨタカ
  cn:林夜鹰
Caprimulgus affinis

Drawing J.G.Keulemans

Swifts - *Apodidae*

The family of Swifts is globally distributed except in the coldest regions. They are small birds, 9 cm to 23 cm long. The wings are long and pointed, the legs and feet are very small and the beak is small with a crooked point and a wide throat. Sails are perfectly adapted to life in the air, and some species are able to spend the night in flight and to mate. They are excellent and fast fliers, on the other hand, many species cannot take off from the ground. The nests of a few species are made entirely of saliva and are considered a delicacy in Chinese cuisine. Some species of salangan have the exceptional echolocation capability. They use this to orient themselves in underground cave systems, where their nesting sites are.

adult

S3.0
White-throated Needletail
  de:Stachelschwanzsegler
  fr: Martinet épineux
  es:Vencejo Mongol
  ja:ハリオアマツバメ
  cn:白喉针尾雨燕
Hirundapus caudacutus

Photo Aviceda

Silver-backed Needletail
de:Graukehlsegler
fr: Martinet de Cochinchine
es: Vencejo de la Cochinchina
ja: クロビタイハリオアマツバメ
cn:白背针尾雨燕
Hirundapus cochinchinensis

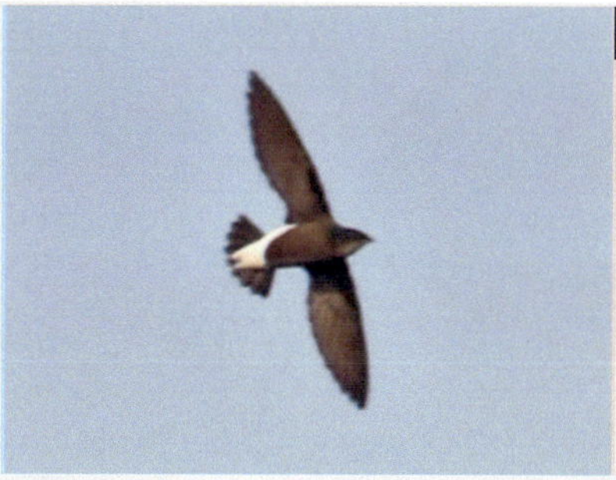

adult
S4.0
Photo TonyCastro

Brown-backed Needletail
de:Eilsegler
fr: Martinet géant
es: Vencejo Gigante
ja: オオハリオアマツバメ
cn:褐背针尾雨燕
Hirundapus giganteus

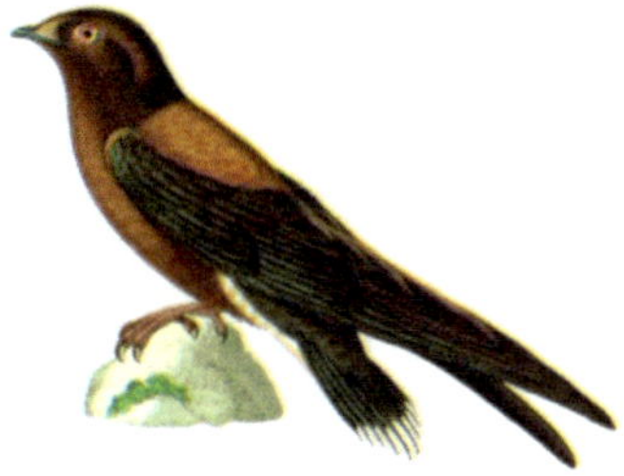

adult
PD
Drawing Huet

Himalayan Swiftlet
de:Himalayasalangane
fr: Salangane de l'Himalaya
es: Rabitojo Himalayo
ja: ヒマラヤアナツバメ
cn:短嘴金丝燕
Aerodramus brevirostris

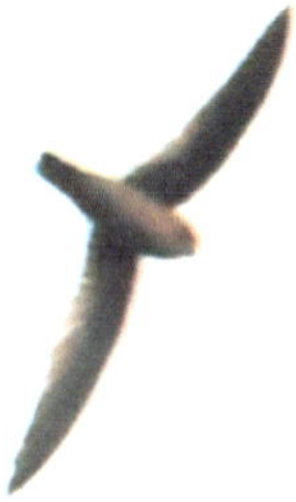

adult
S4.0
Photo TonyCastro

Black-nest Swiftlet
de:Schwarznestsalangane
fr: Salangane à nid noir
es: Salangana Nidonegro
ja: オオアナツバメ
cn:大金丝燕
Aerodramus maximus

adult
S2.0
Photo wokoti

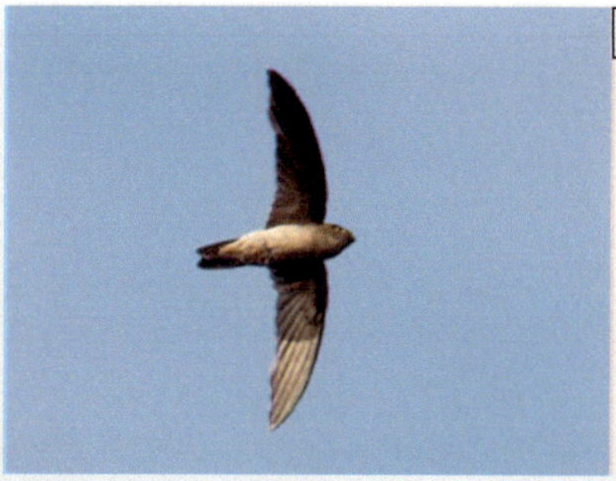

adult

A2.0 **Germain's Swiftlet**
de:Oustaletsalangane
fr: Salangane de German
es: Rabitojo de Oustalet
ja: ジャワナツバメ
cn:淡腰金丝燕
Aerodramus germani

adult

S3.0 **Fork-tailed Swift**
de:Pazifiksegler
fr: Martinet de Sibérie
es: Vencejo del Pacífico
ja: アマツバメ
cn:白腰雨燕
Apus pacificus

adult

AU **Cook's Swift**
de:Cooksegler
fr: Martinet de Cook
es: Vencejo de Cook
ja: クックアマツバメ
cn:库氏雨燕
Apus cooki

adult

PD **House Swift**
de:Malaiensegler
fr: Martinet malais
es: Vencejo Oriental
ja: ヒメアマツバメ
cn:小白腰雨燕
Apus nipalensis

Asian Palm Swift
  de:Bengalensegler
  fr: Martinet batassia
  es: Vencejo Palmero Asiático
  ja:アジアヤシアマツバメ
  cn:棕雨燕
Cypsiurus balasiensis

adult

Tree-swifts - *Hemiprocnidae*

The only four species of the family of Treeswifts are found only in Southeast Asia from India to the Solomon Islands. The body size ranges from 15 cm to 33 cm. The slender birds have long, pointed wings and a long forked tail. Unlike the true swifts, their hind toe is non-reversible. Their habitat are tree-lined landscapes. They are mostly in the air, but also sit on trees. They only feed on insects that they catch in flight. The nest is made of hardened saliva and feathers that are glued to a branch high in the tree. The nest is so small and fragile that the incubating adult bird can only sit on the branch and not on the nest. The only egg is incubated by both parents and the altricial chick is looked after by both parents.

Crested Treeswift
  de:Kronenbaumsegler
  fr: Hémiprocné couronné
  es: Vencejo Arborícola Coronado
  ja: インドカンムリアマツバメ
  cn:凤头雨燕
Hemiprocne coronata

♂ adult

Trogons - *Trogonidae*

Trogons are among the most beautiful birds in the world. Particularly noticeable is the quetzal, whose two central tail coverts can reach more than three times the body length of 38 cm. It was revered as a sacred bird by the Aztecs and Mayans and is now the national bird of Guatemala. The smallest species is the Black-throated Trogon from Central and South America with a body length of 23 cm, the largest species is Ward's Trogon with 40 cm from East Asia. Trogons occur up to an altitude of 3600 m. The nests of the trogons with up to 4 eggs are created in existing caves. All trogons catch insects in flight or pick fruits and caterpillars from leaves or branches.

♂ adult

Drawing J.Gould&H.C.Richter

PD

Red-headed Trogon
de:Rotkopftrogon
fr: Trogon à tête rouge
es: Trogón Cabecirrojo
ja: ズアカキヌバネドリ
cn:红头咬鹃
Harpactes erythrocephalus

♂ adult

Drawing J.G.Keulemans

PD

Orange-breasted Trogon
de:Orangebrusttrogon
fr: Trogon à poitrine jaune
es: Trogón Pechinaranja
ja: ヤマキヌバネドリ
cn:橙胸咬鹃
Harpactes oreskios

♂ adult

Drawing H.Groenvold

PD

Ward's Trogon
de:Rosenschwanztrogon
fr: Trogon de Ward
es: Trogón de Ward
ja: ビルマキヌバネドリ
cn:红腹咬鹃
Harpactes wardi
Near threatened.

Hoopoes - *Upupidae*

The family of Hoopoes is found in Eurasia and Africa and they are migratory birds. The body length is 16 cm to 32 cm. A hoopoe has broad round wings and a long squared tail. The third and fourth toes are fused at the root. The beak is long, slender and curved downwards. The feather crest can be erected and has black tips. They feed on insects and other invertebrates, but also on small vertebrates. They nest in a cave. The female breeds alone and is fed by the male.

Eurasian Hoopoe
  de: Wiedehopf
  fr: Huppe fasciée
  es: Abubilla
  ja: ヤツガシラ
  cn: 戴胜
Upupa epops

  www.avitopia.net/bird.en/?vid=2075101
  www.avitopia.net/bird.en/?wid=2075101

adult

Hornbills - *Bucerotidae*

The family of Hornbills is found in tropical areas of Asia and sub-Saharan Africa. The body length of the birds is from 32 cm to 140 cm. Most species have a casque on their upper mandible. They live in forests and are tree dwellers and diurnal omnivores. The nests are created in holes or crevices, with the female walling herself in with mud or droppings, leaving only a small opening through which the male can transfer food. The young hatch after 30 to 50 days of incubation; during this time the female molts.

Great Hornbill
  de: Doppelhornvogel
  fr: Calao bicorne
  es: Cálao Bicorne
  ja: オオサイチョウ
  cn: 双角犀鸟
Buceros bicornis
Near threatened.

adult

♂ adult

Photo Atsuo Tsuji

S4.0

Austen's Hornbill
  de:Weißgesicht-Hornvogel
  fr: Calao d'Austen
  es: Cálao Pardo de Austen
  ja: アッサムサイチョウ
  cn: 白喉犀鸟
Anorrhinus austeni
Near threatened.

♂ adult

Photo J.Mosesso

PD

Oriental Pied Hornbill
  de:Orienthornvogel
  fr: Calao pie
  es: Cálao Cariblanco
  ja: キタカササギサイチョウ
  cn: 冠斑犀鸟
Anthracoceros albirostris

♂

Photo Morton Strange

S4.0

Rufous-necked Hornbill
  de:Nepalhornvogel
  fr: Calao à cou roux
  es: Cálao del Nepal
  ja: ナナミゾサイチョウ
  cn: 棕颈犀鸟
Aceros nipalensis
Vulnerable.

♂♀ adult

Drawing J.G.Keulemans

PD

Wreathed Hornbill
  de:Furchenhornvogel
  fr: Calao festonné
  es: Cálao Gorginegro
  ja: シワコブサイチョウ
  cn: 花冠皱盔犀鸟
Rhyticeros undulatus

Kingfishers - *Alcedinidae*

The family of Kingfishers are found worldwide except in the coldest areas and some islands. They are between 10 and 45 cm long. Kingfishers have a stocky body, short wings, and tiny to very long tails. The head is large, the neck short, and the beak long and thick. When hunting, they come down from a viewing point. Some species are capable of hovering flight. They breed in caves.

Blyth's Kingfisher
de:Herkuleseisvogel
fr: Martin-pêcheur de Blyth
es: Martín Pescador Hércules
ja: オオカワセミ
cn:斑头大翠鸟
Alcedo hercules
Near threatened.

♂ adult

Common Kingfisher
de:Eisvogel
fr: Martin-pêcheur d'Europe
es: Martín Pescador Común
ja: カワセミ
cn:普通翠鸟
Alcedo atthis

♂ adult

Blue-eared Kingfisher
de:Menintingeisvogel
fr: Martin-pêcheur méninting
es: Martín Pescador Meninting
ja: ルリカワセミ
cn:蓝耳翠鸟
Alcedo meninting

adult

adult

PD Oriental Dwarf Kingfisher
de:Dschungelfischer
fr: Martin-pêcheur pourpré
es: Martín Pescador Enano Oriental
ja: ミツユビカワセミ
cn:三趾翠鸟
Ceyx erithaca

♂ adult

PD Banded Kingfisher
de:Wellenliest
fr: Martin-chasseur mignon
es: Martín Cazador Chico
ja: カザリショウビン
cn:横斑翠鸟
Lacedo pulchella

adult

PD Stork-billed Kingfisher
de:Storchschnabelliest
fr: Martin-chasseur gurial
es: Alción Picocigüeña
ja: コウハシショウビン
cn:鹳嘴翡翠
Pelargopsis capensis

adult

PD Ruddy Kingfisher
de:Feuerliest
fr: Martin-chasseur violet
es: Alción Rojizo
ja: アカショウビン
cn:赤翡翠
Halcyon coromanda

White-throated Kingfisher
  de:Braunliest
  fr: Martin-chasseur de Smyrne
  es: Alción de Esmirna
  ja: アオショウビン
  cn:白胸翡翠
Halcyon smyrnensis

adult

Black-capped Kingfisher
  de:Kappenliest
  fr: Martin-chasseur à coiffe noire
  es: Alción Capirotado
  ja: ヤマショウビン
  cn:蓝翡翠
Halcyon pileata

adult

Collared Kingfisher
  de:Halsbandliest
  fr: Martin-chasseur à collier blanc
  es: Alción Acollarado
  ja: ナンヨウショウビン
  cn:白领翡翠
Todiramphus chloris

adult

Crested Kingfisher
  de:Trauerfischer
  fr: Martin-pêcheur tacheté
  es: Martín Gigante Asiático
  ja: ヤマセミ
  cn:冠鱼狗
Megaceryle lugubris

adult

AU

Pied Kingfisher
de:Graufischer
fr: Martin-pêcheur pie
es: Martín Pescador Pío
ja: ヒメヤマセミ
cn: 斑鱼狗
Ceryle rudis

Photo W.J.Daunicht

adult

Bee-eaters - *Meropidae*

The family of bee-eaters occurs in tropical and subtropical areas on all continents of the Old World. The body length of the birds is 15 cm to 35 cm. The body is slender, the wings long and pointed, the tail is long, the legs and fused toes are slender. The long beak is compressed at the side and bent. The plumage is very different, with the bright colors red and green predominate. Most species are good fliers and snap their food, including bees and wasps, in the air. Many nest in colonies, both parents dig a tunnel up to one meter long in an embankment that ends in a small chamber. 2 to 5 eggs are laid there.

PD

Blue-bearded Bee-eater
de:Blaubartspint
fr: Guêpier à barbe bleue
es: Abejaruco Barbiazul
ja: アオムネハチクイ
cn: 蓝须夜蜂虎
Nyctyornis athertoni

Drawing J.G.Keulemans

adult

AU

Green Bee-eater
de:Smaragdspint
fr: Guêpier d'Orient
es: Abejaruco Esmeralda
ja: ミドリハチクイ
cn: 绿喉蜂虎
Merops orientalis

Photo W.J.Daunicht

adult

Blue-throated Bee-eater
de:Malaienspint
fr: Guêpier à gorge bleue
es: Abejaruco Gorgiazul
ja:ルリノドハチクイ
cn:蓝喉蜂虎
Merops viridis

adult

Blue-tailed Bee-eater
de:Blauschwanzspint
fr: Guêpier à queue d'azur
es: Abejaruco Coliazul
ja:ハリオハチクイ
cn:栗喉蜂虎
Merops philippinus

adult

Chestnut-headed Bee-eater
de:Braunkopfspint
fr: Guêpier de Leschenault
es: Abejaruco Cabecirrufo
ja:チャガシラハチクイ
cn:栗头蜂虎
Merops leschenaulti

adult

Rollers - *Coraciidae*

The family of Rollers occurs in the warmer areas of the Old World, and in some cases they are downright long-distance migrants. The body length is 25 cm to 40 cm. They have long wings and a long tail that is often forked or notched. The beak is broad and hook-shaped. The plumage of most species is brightly colored. The voice is harsh, unmelodious and not very variable. They are good fliers, but like to hunt from a perch. Their courtship display in the air is spectacular and involves rolling. They nest in cavities.

adult

Indian Roller
  de:Hinduracke
  fr: Rollier indien
  es:Carraca India
  ja: インドブッポウソウ
  cn:棕胸佛法僧
Coracias benghalensis

adult

Oriental Dollarbird
  de:Türkisracke
  fr: Rolle oriental
  es:Carraca Oriental
  ja:ブッポウソウ
  cn:三宝鸟
Eurystomus orientalis

Asian Barbets - *Megalaimidae*

The family of Asian Barbets is restricted to the Indomalayan region. They become 15 cm to 30 cm long. They look a bit plump and have large beaks that are surrounded by bristles. Their habitat is the interior of forests. They contribute to the spread of seeds by eating fruit whole and later regurgitate indigestible material. But they also eat a wide variety of small animals. They nest in caves that they bore into trees. They lay 2 to 4 eggs, which they incubate for 13 to 15 days.

Coppersmith Barbet
de:Kupferschmied
fr: Barbu à plastron rouge
es: Barbudo Calderero
ja: ムネアカゴシキドリ
cn:赤胸拟䴕
Psilopogon haemacephalus

adult

Blue-eared Barbet
de:Schwarzohr-Bartvogel
fr: Barbu à oreillons noirs
es: Barbudo orejinegro
ja: アオミミゴシキドリ
cn:蓝耳拟啄木鸟
Psilopogon duvaucelii

adult

Great Barbet
de:Heulbartvogel
fr: Barbu géant
es: Barbudo Grande
ja: オオゴシキドリ
cn:大拟䴕
Psilopogon virens

adult

Drawing H.Groenvold

Drawing H.Groenvold

Drawing J.G.Keulemans

adult

PD Red-vented Barbet
de:Rotsteiß-Bartvogel
fr: Barbu à ventre rouge
es: Barbudo Ventrirrojo
ja: シリアカオオゴシキドリ
cn:红臀拟鴷
Psilopogon lagrandieri

Drawing Huet

adult

PD Green-eared Barbet
de:Grünohr-Bartvogel
fr: Barbu grivelé
es: Barbudo Orejiverde
ja: ミミアオゴシキドリ
cn:黄纹拟鴷
Psilopogon faiostrictus

Drawing Pretre

adult

PD Lineated Barbet
de:Streifenbartvogel
fr: Barbu rayé
es: Barbudo Listado
ja: シロボシオオゴシキドリ
cn:纹拟鴷
Psilopogon lineatus

Drawing J.G.Keulemans

adult

PD Golden-throated Barbet
de:Goldkehl-Bartvogel
fr: Barbu de Franklin
es: Barbudo de Franklin
ja: キンノドゴシキドリ
cn:金喉拟鴷
Psilopogon franklinii

Drawing H.Groenvold

Moustached Barbet

de: Grünscheitel-Bartvogel
fr: Barbu de Hume
es: Barbudo Bigotudo
ja: クロヒゲゴシキドリ
cn: 休氏拟鹦

Psilopogon incognitus

♂♀ adult

Drawing G.S

Blue-throated Barbet

de: Blauwangen-Bartvogel
fr: Barbu à gorge bleue
es: Barbudo Gorgiazul
ja: アオノドゴシキドリ
cn: 蓝喉拟

Psilopogon asiaticus

adult

Drawing J.G.Keulemans

Indochinese Barbet

de: Annambartvogel
fr: Barbu d'Annam
es: Barbudo de Annam
ja: インドシナゴシキドリ
cn: 印支拟啄木鸟

Psilopogon annamensis

adult

Drawing W.J.Daunicht

Woodpeckers - *Picidae*

The family of Woodpeckers is found worldwide, but not in Madagascar, Australia and most of the Indonesian islands. The body length ranges from 9 cm to 60 cm. The feet have 3 or 4 toes, two of which point forward. They have a chunky head and a straight, usually powerful beak. The sexes are mostly different. Woodpeckers mostly inhabit trees. Most species feed on insects, which they pull out with their long and flexible tongue. When climbing vertical logs, the stiff tail serves as a support. They make a cave in a tree to breed.

Photo Martien Brand

adult

Eurasian Wryneck
de:Wendehals
fr: Torcol fourmilier
es:Torcecuello Euroasiático
ja:アリスイ
cn:蟻鴷
Jynx torquilla

Drawing J.Gould&H.C.Richter

♂ adult

Speckled Piculet
de:Tüpfelzwergspecht
fr: Picumne tacheté
es:Carpinterito Moteado
ja:アジアヒメキツツキ
cn:斑姬啄木鸟
Picumnus innominatus

Drawing J.Gould&H.C.Richter

♂ adult

White-browed Piculet
de:Rötelmausspecht
fr: Picumne à sourcils blancs
es:Carpinterito Cejiblanco
ja:インドミツユビコゲラ
cn:白眉棕啄木鸟
Sasia ochracea

Grey-capped Pygmy Woodpecker
de:Grauscheitelspecht
fr: Pic à coiffe grise
es: Pico Crestigrís
ja: ハイガシラコゲラ
cn:星头啄木鸟
Dendrocopos canicapillus

AU

Photo W.J.Daunicht

adult

Freckle-breasted Woodpecker
de:Sprenkelbrustspecht
fr: Pic de Bonaparte
es: Pico pechimoteado
ja: ムナホシアカゲラ
cn:雀斑胸啄木鸟
Dendrocopos analis

PD

Drawing P.Oudart

♂ adult

Stripe-breasted Woodpecker
de:Streifenbrustspecht
fr: Pic à poitrine rayée
es: Pico Estriado
ja: ムナフアカゲラ
cn:纹胸啄木鸟
Dendrocopos atratus

PD

Drawing J.G.Keulemans

♂♀ adult

Yellow-crowned Woodpecker
de:Gelbscheitelspecht
fr: Pic mahratte
es: Pico Mahratta
ja: ベンガルアカゲラ
cn:黄冠啄木鸟
Dendrocopos mahrattensis

PD

Drawing J.&E.Gould

♂ adult

adult

AU

Rufous-bellied Woodpecker

  de:Braunkehlspecht

  fr: Pic à ventre fauve

  es:Pico Ventrirrufo

  ja:チャバラアカゲラ

  cn:棕腹啄木鸟

Dendrocopos hyperythrus

adult

PD

Crimson-breasted Woodpecker

  de:Rotbrustspecht

  fr: Pic à plastron rouge

  es:Pico Pechirrojo

  ja:ヒムネアカゲラ

  cn:赤胸啄木鸟

Dendrocopos cathpharius

♂ adult

PD

Darjeeling Woodpecker

  de:Darjeelingspecht

  fr: Pic de Darjiling

  es:Pico de Darjeeling

  ja:キバラアカゲラ

  cn:黄颈啄木鸟

Dendrocopos darjellensis

♂ adult

AU

Great Spotted Woodpecker

  de:Buntspecht

  fr: Pic épeiche

  es:Pico Picapinos

  ja:アカゲラ

  cn:大斑啄木鸟

Dendrocopos major

www.avitopia.net/bird.en/?vid=2526120

www.avitopia.net/bird.en/?wid=2526120

www.avitopia.net/bird.en/?aud=2526120

White-bellied Woodpecker
de: Weißbauchspecht
fr: Pic à ventre blanc
es: Picamaderos Ventriblanco
ja: キタタキ
cn: 白腹黑啄木鸟
Dryocopus javensis

Drawing J.G.Keulemans

♂ adult

Lesser Yellownape
de: Gelbhaubenspecht
fr: Pic à huppe jaune
es: Pito Crestigualdo
ja: ヒメアオゲラ
cn: 黄冠啄木鸟
Picus chlorolophus

Drawing H.Groenvold

♂ adult

Greater Yellownape
de: Gelbnackenspecht
fr: Pic à nuque jaune
es: Pito Nuquigualdo
ja: キエリアオゲラ
cn: 人黄冠啄木鸟
Picus flavinucha

Drawing J.Gould&H.C.Richter

♂♀ adult

Laced Woodpecker
de: Netzbauchspecht
fr: Pic médiastin
es: Pito Colinegro
ja: タケアオゲラ
cn: 花腹绿啄木鸟
Picus vittatus

Photo W.J.Daunicht

♂ adult

♂ adult

PD **Streak-throated Woodpecker**
de:Schuppenbauchspecht
fr: Pic striolé
es:Pito Culigualdo
ja: ムナフタケアオゲラ
cn:鳞喉绿啄木鸟
Picus xanthopygaeus

♂ adult

PD **Red-collared Woodpecker**
de:Halsbandspecht
fr: Pic de Rabier
es:Pito Vietnamita
ja: アンナンヤマゲラ
cn:红颈绿啄木鸟
Picus rabieri
Near threatened.

♂ adult

PD **Black-headed Woodpecker**
de:Rotbürzelspecht
fr: Pic à tête noire
es:Pito Cabecinegro
ja: コシアカアオゲラ
cn:黑头绿啄木鸟
Picus erythropygius

♂ adult

S3.0 **Grey-headed Woodpecker**
de:Grauspecht
fr: Pic cendré
es:Pito Cano
ja: ヤマゲラ
cn:灰头绿啄木鸟
Picus canus

Common Goldenback
de:Feuerrückenspecht
fr: Pic à dos rouge
es: Pito Culirrojo
ja: ズアカミユビゲラ
cn:金背三趾啄木鸟
Dinopium javanense

♂ adult

Pale-headed Woodpecker
de:Blasskopf-Bambusspecht
fr: Pic grantia
es: Pito del Bambú Norteño
ja: タケゲラ
cn:苍头竹啄木鸟
Gecinulus grantia

♂ adult

Rufous Woodpecker
de:Rötelspecht
fr: Pic brun
es: Carpintero Rufo
ja: クリチャゲラ
cn:栗啄木鸟
Micropternus brachyurus

♂ adult

Black-and-buff Woodpecker
de:Dommelspecht
fr: Pic à jugulaire
es: Pito Blanquinegro
ja: クロカレハゲラ
cn:黑棕斑啄木鸟
Meiglyptes jugularis

adult

♂ adult

PD **Greater Flameback**
de:Goldmantel-Sultanspecht
fr: Pic de Tickell
es:Pito sultán grande
ja:オオコガネゲラ
cn:大金背啄木鸟
Chrysocolaptes guttacristatus

♂♀ adult

PD **Bay Woodpecker**
de:Rotohrspecht
fr: Pic à oreillons rouges
es:Pito Orejirrojo
ja:ヤブゲラ
cn:黄嘴栗啄木鸟
Blythipicus pyrrhotis

♂ adult

PD **Heart-spotted Woodpecker**
de:Rundschwanzspecht
fr: Pic canente
es:Pito de Corazones
ja:クロカンムリコゲラ
cn:黑冠啄木鸟
Hemicircus canente

♂ adult

AU **Great Slaty Woodpecker**
de:Puderspecht
fr: Pic meunier
es:Picatroncos Pizarroso
ja:ボウシゲラ
cn:大灰啄木鸟
Mulleripicus pulverulentus
Vulnerable.

Falcons - *Falconidae*

The family of Falcons is found on every continent except Antarctica. Their length ranges from 15 cm to 65 cm. Hawks have long, pointed wings, a half-length tail and short legs that end in long toes with curved claws. The beak is short and usually has a so-called 'falcon tooth' in the upper beak. The flight is determined and fast. Some species strike their prey in flight after a chase, while other species take them on the ground after diving. In fact, the fastest fliers among birds belong to this family.

White-rumped Falcon
de: Langschwanz-Zwergfalke
fr: Fauconnet à pattes jaunes
es: Halconcito Asiático
ja: アジアコビトハヤブサ
cn: 白腰侏隼
Polihierax insignis
Near threatened.

♀ adult

Drawing J.G.Keulemans

PD

Collared Falconet
de: Rotkehlfälkchen
fr: Fauconnet à collier
es: Falconete Acollarado
ja: モモアカヒメハヤブサ
cn: 紅腿小隼
Microhierax caerulescens

adult

Drawing H.Groenvold

PD

Pied Falconet
de: Elsterfälkchen
fr: Fauconnet noir et blanc
es: Falconete Pío
ja: シロハラヒメハヤブサ
cn: 白腿小隼
Microhierax melanoleucos

adult

Drawing H.Groenvold

PD

Photo W.J.Daunicht

♂ adult

AU Common Kestrel
de:Turmfalke
fr: Faucon crécerelle
es: Cernícalo Vulgar
ja: チョウゲンボウ
cn:红隼

Falco tinnunculus

🔊 www.avitopia.net/bird.en/?kom=2576102
▢ www.avitopia.net/bird.en/?vid=2576102
🔊 www.avitopia.net/bird.en/?aud=2576102

Photo W.J.Daunicht

♂ adult

AU Amur Falcon
de:Amurfalke
fr: Faucon de l'Amour
es: Cernícalo del Amur
ja: アカアシチョウゲンボウ
cn:红脚隼

Falco amurensis

Photo Dwayne

♂ adult

A2.0 Merlin
de:Merlin
fr: Faucon émerillon
es: Esmerejón
ja: コチョウゲンボウ
cn:灰背隼

Falco columbarius

Drawing J.G.Keulemans

♂ adult

PD Eurasian Hobby
de:Baumfalke
fr: Faucon hobereau
es: Alcotán Europeo
ja: チゴハヤブサ
cn:燕隼

Falco subbuteo

Oriental Hobby
  de:Malaienbaumfalke
  fr: Faucon aldrovandin
  es:Alcotán Filipino
  ja:ミナミチゴハヤブサ
  cn:猛隼
Falco severus

adult

Peregrine Falcon
  de:Wanderfalke
  fr: Faucon pèlerin
  es:Halcón Peregrino
  ja:ハヤブサ
  cn:游隼
Falco peregrinus

adult

Old World Parrots - *Psittaculidae*

This family is limited to the warm areas of the 'Old World'. It consists of the five subfamilies Agapornithinae, Loriinae, Platycercinae, Psittacellinae and Psittaculinae. The body length ranges from 10 cm to 50 cm. The legs are short, two toes are pointing forward and two are pointing backward with strong claws. The beak is strong and strongly curved. They nest in hollows and less often in crevices.

Alexandrine Parakeet
  de:Großer Alexandersittich
  fr: Perruche alexandre
  es:Cotorra Alejandrina
  ja:オオホンセイインコ
  cn:阿历山大鹦鹉
Psittacula eupatria
Near threatened.

♂ adult

♂ adult

AU

Rose-ringed Parakeet
de:Halsbandsittich
fr: Perruche à collier
es:Cotorra de Kramer
ja:ホンセイインコ
cn:红领绿鹦鹉
Psittacula krameri
Introduced.

🔊 www.avitopia.net/bird.en/?kom=2651103

♂♀ adult

PD

Grey-headed Parakeet
de:Finschsittich
fr: Perruche de Finsch
es:Cotorra de Finsch
ja:ズグロコセイインコ
cn:灰头鹦鹉
Psittacula finschii
Near threatened.

adult

AU

Blossom-headed Parakeet
de:Rosenkopfsittich
fr: Perruche à tête rose
es:Cotorra Carirrosa
ja:バライロコセイインコ
cn:花头鹦鹉
Psittacula roseata
Near threatened.

adult

AU

Red-breasted Parakeet
de:Bartsittich
fr: Perruche à moustaches
es:Cotorra Pechirroja
ja:ダルマインコ
cn:绯胸鹦鹉
Psittacula alexandri
Near threatened.

Vernal Hanging Parrot
de:Frühlingspapageichen
fr: Coryllis vernal
es:Lorículo Vernal
ja: ミドリサトウチョウ
cn:短尾鹦鹉
Loriculus vernalis

adult

Broadbills - *Eurylaimidae*

The family of Broadbills occurs in Southeast Asia from the eastern Himalayas to the Philippines. The body length ranges from 13 cm to 28 cm. They have broad heads, large eyes, and flat broad bills. Their habitat is the dense canopies of rainforests. They are insectivores and carnivores. The pear-shaped nests often hang above water on branches or vines.

Black-and-red Broadbill
de:Kellenschnabel
fr: Eurylaime rouge et noir
es:Eurilaimo Rojinegro
ja: クロアカヒロハシ
cn:黑红阔嘴鸟
Cymbirhynchus macrorhynchos

adult

Long-tailed Broadbill
de:Papageibreitrachen
fr: Eurylaime psittacin
es:Eurilaimo Lorito
ja: オナガヒロハシ
cn:长尾阔嘴鸟
Psarisomus dalhousiae

adult

adult

PD **Silver-breasted Broadbill**
de:Würgerbreitrachen
fr: Eurylaime de Gould
es:Eurilaimo Pechoplata
ja:ギンムネヒロハシ
cn:银胸丝冠鸟
Serilophus lunatus

adult

S2.0 **Banded Broadbill**
de:Rosenkopf-Breitrachen
fr: Eurylaime de Horsfield
es:Eurilaimo Bandeado
ja:アズキヒロハシ
cn:斑阔嘴鸟
Eurylaimus javanicus

adult

PD **Dusky Broadbill**
de:Riesenbreitrachen
fr: Eurylaime corydon
es:Eurilaimo Sombrío
ja: ガマヒロハシ
cn:暗阔嘴鸟
Corydon sumatranus

Pittas - *Pittidae*

The family of Pittas can be found in Central and South Africa, Southeast Asia and Northern Australia. The birds are bulky, have short wings, short tails and long legs. The neck is short and the beak strong. The body length ranges from 15 cm to 30 cm. The plumage has iridescent colors. Despite the bright colors, they are secret ground dwellers and not easy to spot. Their diet consists of small animals and fruits. the large covered nest made of twigs, leaves and roots has a side entrance. The 3 to 7 eggs and the nidicolous young are incubated and looked after by both parents.

Eared Pitta
  de:Sichelpitta
  fr: Brève ornée
  es: Pita Orejuda
  ja: ツノヤイロチョウ
  cn:双辫八色鸫
Hydrornis phayrei

♂♀ adult

Rusty-naped Pitta
  de:Braunkopfpitta
  fr: Brève à nuque fauve
  es: Pita Rojiza
  ja: チャガシラヤイロチョウ
  cn:栗头八色鸫
Hydrornis oatesi

♂ adult

Blue-naped Pitta
  de:Blaunackenpitta
  fr: Brève à nuque bleue
  es: Pita Nuquiazul
  ja: アオエリヤイロチョウ
  cn:蓝枕八色鸫
Hydrornis nipalensis

♂ adult

Drawing W.M.Hart
Drawing W.M.Hart
Drawing J.Gould&H.C.Richter
PD

♂ adult

Drawing W.M.Hart

PD **Blue-rumped Pitta**
de:Blaubürzelpitta
fr: Brève à dos bleu
es: Pita Lomiazul
ja: コシアオヤイロチョウ
cn:蓝背八色鸫
Hydrornis soror

♂ adult

Drawing J.Gould&H.C.Richter

PD **Blue Pitta**
de:Blaupitta
fr: Brève bleue
es: Pita Azul
ja: ルリヤイロチョウ
cn:蓝八色鸫
Hydrornis cyaneus

♂ adult

Drawing H.Groenvold

PD **Bar-bellied Pitta**
de:Elliotpitta
fr: Brève d'Elliot
es: Pita de Elliot
ja: ミドリシマヤイロチョウ
cn:斑腹八色鸫
Hydrornis elliotii

adult

Photo W.J.Daunicht

AU **Blue-winged Pitta**
de:Blauflügelpitta
fr: Brève à ailes bleues
es: Pita Aliazul
ja: ミナミヤイロチョウ
cn:马来八色鸫
Pitta moluccensis

www.avitopia.net/bird.en/?vid=2825304
www.avitopia.net/bird.en/?wid=2825304

Fairy Pitta
  de:Nymphenpitta
  fr: Brève migratrice
  es: Pita Ninfa
  ja: ヤイロチョウ
  cn:仙八色鸫
Pitta nympha
Vulnerable.

adult

Hooded Pitta
  de:Kappenpitta
  fr: Brève à capuchon
  es: Pita Encapuchada
  ja: ズグロヤイロチョウ
  cn:绿胸八色鸫
Pitta sordida

adult

Thornbills and Gerygones - *Acanthizidae*

The family of the Thornbills and Gerygones occurs in Australasia from Myanmar to Australia to New Zealand. Their body length is between 8 cm and 19 cm. They have short rounded wings, slender bills, long legs and a short tail. Their habitat is woodland or scrubland. Most species are terrestrial, some species live in treetops, another in rocky landscapes. They feed mainly on insects, only a few on seeds or fruits. They lay 1 to 4 eggs and the breeding season is exceptionally long for passerines, up to 24 days. However, hatching takes place completely simultaneously.

Golden-bellied Gerygone
  de:Goldbrustgerygone
  fr: Gérygone soufrée
  es: Ratona Hada de Vientre Dorado
  ja: マレアシアセンニョムシクイ
  cn:黄胸噪刺莺
Gerygone sulphurea

adult

Vangas - *Vangidae*

The family of Vangas occurs in Madagascar, Africa and Asia. It has been rearranged based on recent research. They look very different, which is why it has not been immediately recognized, that they belong to a common family. Their body length ranges from 12 cm to 32 cm. They are predominantly insectivores.

adult

Large Woodshrike
de:Großer Raupenwürger
fr: Téphrodorne bridé
es:Minivete de Cola Castaña
ja: オオモズサンショウクイ
cn:钩嘴林鵙
Tephrodornis virgatus

adult

Common Woodshrike
de:Kleiner Raupenwürger
fr: Téphrodorne de Pondichéry
es:Minivete Común
ja: モズサンショウクイ
cn:林鵙
Tephrodornis pondicerianus

adult

Bar-winged Flycatcher-shrike
de:Elsterraupenschmätzer
fr: Échenilleur gobemouche
es:Minivete de Alas Barreadas
ja: ヒタキサンショウクイ
cn:褐背鹟鵙
Hemipus picatus

Rufous-winged Philentoma
  de:Kastanienflügelschnäpper
  fr: Philentome à ailes rousses
  es:Monarca de Alas Castañas
  ja:チャバネアカメヒタキ
  cn:棕翅王鹟
Philentoma pyrhoptera

♂ adult

Woodswallows - *Artamidae*

The family of Woodswallows occurs from India and Australia to the Fiji Islands. The body size ranges from 15 cm to 20 cm. They are persistent fliers and, besides the ravens, the only songbirds that can sail for a long time. Their habitat are open landscapes and light forests. They live on insects, which they catch like swallows or like flycatchers from a perch. Starlings are gregarious and aggressive and also attack larger birds. Their nests are flat cup-shaped and are built in a tree or bush, occasionally they nest in colonies. The clutch consists of 2 to 4 eggs, which both parents take care of.

Ashy Woodswallow
  de:Grauschwalbenstar
  fr: Langrayen brun
  es:Golondrina del Bosque Ceniza
  ja:ハイイロモリツバメ
  cn:灰燕鹀
Artamus fuscus

adult

Ioras - *Aegithinidae*

The four species of the family of Ioras are restricted to southern Asia from India to Borneo. The body length ranges from 11.5 cm to 15.5 cm. A special feature are the long, soft feathers on the flanks, which can be erected and are used for courtship and breeding. Their habitat varies greatly and only excludes extremes. They are hightly arborial and usually occur in the tree canopy. They live on fruits and seeds, but insects also play an important role in nutrition. As far as is known, their courtship is quite elaborate. All species build open, cup-shaped nests at least 2 m above ground and lay 2 to 3 eggs. The chicks are altricial.

S3.0

Photo Doug Janson

adult

Common Iora
de:Schwarzflügeliora
fr: Petit Iora
es: Iora Común
ja: ヒメコノハドリ
cn:黑翅雀鹎
Aegithina tiphia

PD

Drawing J.G.Keulemans

♂ adult

Great Iora
de:Großiora
fr: Iora de Lafresnaye
es: Iora Grande
ja: オオヒメコノハドリ
cn:大绿雀鹎
Aegithina lafresnayei

Cuckoo-shrikes - *Campephagidae*

The family of Cuckoo-shrikes is common in the tropics of Africa, Asia, and Australia. The body length is between 13 cm and 30 cm. They are primarily tree dwellers. Most are good fliers and are sociable. They live on insects - especially large hairy caterpillars - and berries. The nest is usually laid out as a flat bowl on a horizontal branch and is sometimes camouflaged with cobwebs and pieces of bark. Both parents take part in the care of the two to four eggs and in the rearing of the young.

Small Minivet
  de:Zwergmennigvogel
  fr: Minivet oranor
  es:Minivete Chico
  ja:コサンショウクイ
  cn:小山椒鸟
Pericrocotus cinnamomeus

♂♀ adult

PD

Drawing J.Gould&H.C.Richter

Grey-chinned Minivet
  de:Graukehl-Mennigvogel
  fr: Minivet mandarin
  es:Minivete de Garganta Amarilla
  ja:ベニサンショウクイ
  cn:灰喉山椒鸟
Pericrocotus solaris

♂ adult

PD

Drawing J.Gould&H.C.Richter

Short-billed Minivet
  de:Kurzschnabel-Mennigvogel
  fr: Minivet à bec court
  es:Minivete de Pico Corto
  ja:コバシベニサンショウクイ
  cn:短嘴山椒鸟
Pericrocotus brevirostris

♂ adult

PD

Drawing J.&E.Gould

Photo J.M.Garg

♂ adult

S3.0 Long-tailed Minivet
de:Langschwanz-Mennigvogel
fr: Minivet rouge
es: Minivete de Cola Larga
ja: オナガベニサンショウクイ
cn:长尾山椒鸟
Pericrocotus ethologus

Drawing J.&E.Gould

♂ adult

PD Scarlet Minivet
de:Scharlachmennigvogel
fr: Minivet écarlate
es: Minivet Escarlata
ja: シュイロサンショウクイ
cn:赤红山椒鸟
Pericrocotus speciosus

Photo Lip Kee Yap

adult

S2.0 Ashy Minivet
de:Graumennigvogel
fr: Minivet cendré
es: Minivete Sombrío
ja: サンショウクイ
cn:灰山椒鸟
Pericrocotus divaricatus

Drawing J.Gould&H.C.Richter

♂ adult

PD Swinhoe's Minivet
de:Braunbürzel-Mennigvogel
fr: Minivet de Swinhoe
es: Minivet de Swinhoe
ja: モモイロサンショウクイ
cn:小灰山椒鸟
Pericrocotus cantonensis

Rosy Minivet

de:Rosenmennigvogel
fr: Minivet rose
es: Minivete Rosado
ja: モモイロサンショウクイ
cn:粉红山椒鸟

Pericrocotus roseus

♂ adult

Drawing J.Gould&H.C.Richter

Large Cuckooshrike

de:Maskenraupenfänger
fr: Échenilleur de Macé
es: Oruguero de Macé
ja: ジャワオニサンショウクイ
cn:大鹃鵙

Coracina macei

♂ adult

Drawing H.Groenvold

Black-winged Cuckooshrike

de:Trauerraupenfänger
fr: Échenilleur ardoisé
es: Oruguero Gris Oscuro
ja: アサクラサンショウクイ
cn:暗灰鹃鵙

Lalage melaschistos

adult

Photo Jason Thompson

Indochinese Cuckooshrike

de:Gartenraupenfänger
fr: Échenilleur indochinois
es: Oruguero de Indochina
ja: ハイイロアサクラサンショウクイ
cn:灰鹃鵙

Lalage polioptera

adult

Drawing J.G.Keulemans

Whistlers - *Pachycephalidae*

The stubborn family occurs in Southeast Asia from India to the islands in the western Pacific. They are about 12 cm to 23 cm tall. Many species have relatively large rounded heads relative to the body. They live in wooded landscapes, especially rainforests. Their diet consists mainly of insects and other invertebrates. This family includes species with an excellent, diverse repertoire of vocalizations, which is also performed with astonishing volume. It is believed that most species are monogamous.

PD Mangrove Whistler
de:Schnäpperdickkopf
fr: Siffleur cendré
es:Silbador de Manglar
ja:マングロアブモズヒタキ
cn:红树啸鹟
Pachycephala cinerea

Drawing Huet

♀ adult

Shrikes - *Laniidae*

The family of Shrikes is found in North America, Eurasia, and Africa. Some species are downright long-distance migrants. The body length ranges from 14 cm to 50 cm. They are slender birds with a long, narrow tail. The head is large with a strong beak with a hook at the tip and tomial teeth on the sides. They are good fliers and very aggressive. From a viewing point they pounce on insects, small reptiles, birds and mammals. They are known to impale their prey on a thorn. The nest is a bowl made of twigs, grass and leaves in a bush or tree.

PD Tiger Shrike
de:Tigerwürger
fr: Pie-grièche tigrine
es: Alcaudón Tigre
ja: チゴモズ
cn:虎纹伯劳
Lanius tigrinus

Drawing J.Smit

♂ adult

Bull-headed Shrike
 de:Büffelkopfwürger
 fr: Pie-grièche bucéphale
 es: Alcaudón Cabeza de Toro
 ja: モズ
 cn:牛头伯劳
Lanius bucephalus

♂ adult

Brown Shrike
 de:Rotschwanzwürger
 fr: Pie-grièche brune
 es: Alcaudón Castaño
 ja: アカモズ
 cn:红尾伯劳
Lanius cristatus

adult

Burmese Shrike
 de:Burmawürger
 fr: Pie-grièche à dos marron
 es: Alcaudón de Burma
 ja: ハイガシラモズ
 cn:栗背伯劳
Lanius collurioides

adult

Long-tailed Shrike
 de:Schachwürger
 fr: Pie-grièche schach
 es: Alcaudón de Cabeza Negra
 ja: タカサゴモズ
 cn:棕背伯劳
Lanius schach

adult

Photo Lip Kee Yap

S2.0

Grey-backed Shrike
de:Tibetwürger
fr: Pie-grièche du Tibet
es: Alcaudón Tibetano
ja: チベットモズ
cn:灰背伯劳
Lanius tephronotus

adult

Vireos and Shrike-Babblers - *Vireonidae*

The family of the Vireos and Shrike-babblers was composed only recently on the basis of DNA studies from the Vireos of America and two genera from the Oriental region. Since they are native to the warm regions, they do not migrate far. They are small birds between 10 cm and 20 cm in length. They live mainly on insects, but also on fruits. They rarely look for food on the ground. The bowl-shaped nest is built hanging in a horizontal fork of a branch.

Drawing J.Gould&H.C.Richter

PD

Black-headed Shrike-Babbler
de:Rotbauch-Würgertimalie
fr: Allotrie à ventre roux
es: Charlatán-Alcaudón de Cabeza Negra
ja: セアカモズチドリ
cn:棕腹鵙鹛
Pteruthius rufiventer

♂ adult

Drawing J.G.Keulemans

PD

Blyth's Shrike-Babbler
de:Blythwürgertimalie
fr: Allotrie siamoise
es: Charlatán-Alcaudón de Blyth
ja: ブライスモズチメドリ
cn:红翅鵙鹛
Pteruthius aeralatus

♂ adult

Dalat Shrike-Babbler
de: Dalatwürgertimalie
fr: Allotrie annamite
es: Charlatán-Alcaudón de Dalat
ja: ダラットズチメドリ
cn: 大叻鵙鹛
Pteruthius annamensis
Endemic.

♂ adult

Drawing W.J.Daunicht — AU

Green Shrike-Babbler
de: Vireowürgertimalie
fr: Allotrie verte
es: Charlatán-Alcaudón Verde
ja: ミドリモズチドリ
cn: 淡绿鵙鹛
Pteruthius xanthochlorus

♂ adult

Drawing J.Gould&H.C.Richter — PD

Black-eared Shrike-Babbler
de: Zimtkehl-Würgertimalie
fr: Allotrie à gorge marron
es: Charlatán-Alcaudón de Orejera Negra
ja: クリノドモズチドリ
cn: 栗喉鵙鹛
Pteruthius melanotis

♂ adult

Drawing J.Gould&H.C.Richter — PD

Clicking Shrike-Babbler
de: Humewürgertimalie
fr: Allotrie de Hume
es: Charlatán-Alcaudón de Hume
ja: インドシナクリビタイモズチメドリ
cn: 栗额鵙鹛
Pteruthius intermedius

adult

Photo Lonelyshrimp — PD

White-bellied Yuhina
de:Grünrückentimalie
fr: Yuhina à ventre blanc
es:Erpornis de Vientre Blanco
ja: アオチメドリ
cn:白腹凤鹛
Erpornis zantholeuca

Drawing J.G.Keulemans

adult

Orioles - *Oriolidae*

The family of Orioles is widespread across all continents of the Old World, with an emphasis on the tropics. Some of the species are migratory birds. They have long wings and a moderately long tail. The body size ranges from 18 cm to 30 cm. The plumage has strong colors, often yellow and black. The sexes are usually different. Some species in New Guinea belonging to the Pitohuis are able to store the poisonous alkaloid batrachotoxin in their plumage and skin in order to defend themselves against parasites and/or predators. Most species build their nests as a hanging bowl high in a tree top.

AU

Black-naped Oriole
de:Schwarznackenpirol
fr: Loriot de Chine
es:Oropéndola de Nuca Negra
ja: コウライウグイス
cn:黑枕黄鹂
Oriolus chinensis

Photo W.J.Daunicht

♂ adult

S4.0

Slender-billed Oriole
de:Dünnschnabelpirol
fr: Loriot à bec effilé
es:Oropéndola Picofino
ja: ミナミコウライウグイス
cn:细嘴黄鹂
Oriolus tenuirostris

Photo Dr Raju Kasambe

♂ adult

Black-hooded Oriole
de: Schwarzkopfpirol
fr: Loriot à capuchon noir
es: Oropéndola de Cabeza Negra Asiática
ja: ズグロコウライウグイス
cn: 黑头黄鹂
Oriolus xanthornus

AU

Photo W.J.Daunicht

adult

Maroon Oriole
de: Blutpirol
fr: Loriot pourpré
es: Oropéndola Marrón
ja: ヒゴロモ
cn: 朱鹂
Oriolus traillii

PD

Drawing J.Wolf

adult

Drongos - *Dicruridae*

The family of Drongos is found in sub-Saharan Africa, Madagascar, southern Asia, Australia, and the Solomon Islands. Their body length ranges from 18 cm to 65 cm. The plumage is black or gray and often shiny, the legs are short and their typical sitting posture is very upright. They live in forests and gardens on trees. They are very good fliers and catch insects in flight or on the ground. They are very aggressive towards predators, so small birds like to build their nests near drongos. The vocalizations are very diverse. Drongos are able to mimic a wide variety of bird calls. They use this ability to use false alarms to induce other birds to flee and thus to give up the current food. The nests are built in a horizontal fork at a great height. The females mainly take care of the offspring.

Photo W.J.Daunicht

AU

Black Drongo
de:Königsdrongo
fr: Drongo royal
es: Drongo Real
ja: オウチュウ
cn:黑卷尾
Dicrurus macrocercus

adult

Photo Lip Kee Yap

S2.0

Ashy Drongo
de:Graudrongo
fr: Drongo cendré
es: Drongo Cenizo
ja: ハイイロオウチュウ
cn:灰卷尾
Dicrurus leucophaeus

adult

Drawing Carl DSilva

Crow-billed Drongo
de:Krähendrongo
fr: Drongo à gros bec
es: Drongo Pico de Cuervo
ja: ハシブトオウチュウ
cn:鸦嘴卷尾
Dicrurus annectans

adult

Bronzed Drongo
  de:Bronzedrongo
  fr: Drongo bronzé
  es: Drongo Bronceado
  ja: ヒメオウチュウ
  cn:古铜色卷尾
Dicrurus aeneus

adult

Lesser Racket-tailed Drongo
  de:Spateldrongo
  fr: Drongo à rames
  es: Drongo de Cola Raqueta Chico
  ja: ヒメカザリオウチュウ
  cn:小盘尾
Dicrurus remifer

adult

Hair-crested Drongo
  de:Haarbuschdrongo
  fr: Drongo à crinière
  es: Drongo Cresta de Pelo
  ja: カンムリオウチュウ
  cn:发冠卷尾
Dicrurus hottentottus

adult

Greater Racket-tailed Drongo
  de:Flaggendrongo
  fr: Drongo à raquettes
  es: Drongo de Cola Raqueta Grande
  ja: カザリオウチュウ
  cn:大盘尾
Dicrurus paradiseus

adult

Fantails - *Rhipiduridae*

The family of Fantails occurs in southeast Australasia from India to the Fiji Islands. The body length ranges from 11.5 cm to 22 cm. Like many other birds - but different from e.g. the drongos (with 10) - they have 12 tail feathers that they often spread. They are very lively and usually hunt insects in flight. Their nests are small and cup-shaped and usually contain 2 to 4 eggs. Both parents take care of the offspring.

adult

Drawing H.Groenvold

PD Pied Fantail
   de:Malaienfächerschwanz
   fr: Rhipidure pie
   es:Cola de Abanico Pálido
   ja: ムナオビオウギビタキ
   cn:斑扇尾鶲
   Rhipidura javanica

adult

Drawing J.G.Keulemans

PD White-throated Fantail
   de:Weißkehl-Fächerschwanz
   fr: Rhipidure à gorge blanche
   es:Cola de Abanico de Garganta Blanca
   ja: ノドジロオウギビタキ
   cn:白喉扇尾鶲
   Rhipidura albicollis

adult

Drawing unknown

PD White-browed Fantail
   de:Weißstirn-Fächerschwanz
   fr: Rhipidure à grands sourcils
   es:Cola de Abanico de Cejas Blancas
   ja: マミジロオウギビタキ
   cn:白眉扇尾鶲
   Rhipidura aureola

Monarchs - *Monarchidae*

The family of Monarch-flycatchers are found in Africa, Asia, Australia and many islands in the Pacific. Most species live in the tropics, only a few extend into the temperate latitudes. Their body length ranges from 9 cm to 50 cm, including elongated tail feathers. They have wide, flat bills and stiff bristles near the nostrils. They are arborial birds and feed mainly on insects and small spiders. Their nests are usually built from plant material in a fork of a branch, only one species builds a mud nest. Some species decorate their nests with lichen.

Black-naped Monarch
de:Schwarzgenickschnäpper
fr: Tchitrec azuré
es: Monarca Azul de Nuca Negra
ja: クロエリヒタキ
cn:黑枕王鶲
Hypothymis azurea

PD

Drawing J.G.Keulemans

adult

Japanese Paradise Flycatcher
de:Japanparadiesschnäpper
fr: Tchitrec du Japon
es: Monarca Paraíso Negro
ja: サンコウチョウ
cn:紫寿帯
Terpsiphone atrocaudata
Near threatened.

PD

Drawing Pretre

♂ adult

Amur Paradise-Flycatcher
de:Amurparadiesschnäpper
fr: Tchitrec de Chine
es: Monarca Paraíso Chino
ja: アムールサンコウチョウ
cn:寿帯
Terpsiphone incei

PD

Drawing J.Gould&H.C.Richter

♂♀ adult

PD Blyth's Paradise-Flycatcher
de:Blythparadiesschnäpper
fr: Tchitrec de Blyth
es: Monarca Paraiso de Blyth
ja: ブライスサンコウチョウ
cn:中南寿带
Terpsiphone affinis

Drawing J.G.Keulemans

adult

Ravens - *Corvidae*

The family of Ravens occurs worldwide with the exception of New Zealand and some islands. The body length is between 18 cm and 70 cm; so among them are the largest of all songbirds. Ravens have powerful bills and often hold the food with their feet when eating. They are curious and one of the most intelligent species in the entire bird world.

AU Eurasian Jay
de:Eichelhäher
fr: Geai des chênes
es: Arrandejo Común
ja: カケス
cn:松鸦
Garrulus glandarius

Photo W.J.Daunicht

www.avitopia.net/bird.en/?kom=4176101
www.avitopia.net/bird.en/?vid=4176101
www.avitopia.net/bird.en/?aud=4176101

adult

PD Yellow-billed Blue Magpie
de:Gelbschnabelkitta
fr: Pirolle à bec jaune
es: Urraca Azul de Pico Amarillo
ja: キバシサンジャク
cn:黄嘴蓝鹊
Urocissa flavirostris

Drawing J.Gould&H.C.Richter

adult

Red-billed Blue Magpie

de:Rotschnabelkitta
fr: Pirolle à bec rouge
es: Urraca Azul de Pico Rojo
ja: サンジャク
cn:红嘴蓝鹊

Urocissa erythroryncha

AU

Photo W.J.Daunicht

adult

White-winged Magpie

de:Graubauchkitta
fr: Pirolle de Whitehead
es: Urraca Azul de Alas Blancas
ja: ハジロサンジャク
cn:白翅蓝鹊

Urocissa whiteheadi

PD

Drawing H.Groenvold

adult

Common Green Magpie

de:Jagdelster
fr: Pirolle verte
es: Urraca Verde
ja: ヘキサン
cn:蓝绿鹊

Cissa chinensis

PD

Drawing J.Gould&H.C.Fichter

adult

Indochinese Green Magpie

de:Goldbauchelster
fr: Pirolle à ventre jaune
es: Urraca Verde Oriental
ja: シナヘキサン
cn:黄胸绿鹊

Cissa hypoleuca

PD

Drawing H.Groenvold

adult

adult

Photo Lip Kee Yap

Rufous Treepie
de:Wanderbaumelster
fr: Témia vagabonde
es: Urraca Vagabunda
ja: チャイロオナガ
cn:棕腹树鹊
Dendrocitta vagabunda

adult

Drawing J.&E.Gould

Grey Treepie
de:Graubrust-Baumelster
fr: Témia de Swinhoe
es: Urraca Himalaya
ja: タイワンオナガ
cn:灰树鹊
Dendrocitta formosae

adult

Drawing D.W.Mitchell

Collared Treepie
de:Maskenbaumelster
fr: Témia masquée
es: Urraca Acollarada
ja: カオグロオナガ
cn:黑额树鹊
Dendrocitta frontalis

adult

Photo W.J.Daunicht

Racket-tailed Treepie
de:Spatelbaumelster
fr: Témia bronzée
es: Urraca Cola de Raqueta Negra
ja: クロラケットオナガ
cn:盘尾树鹊
Crypsirina temia

Ratchet-tailed Treepie
de:Leiterschwanzelster
fr: Témia temnure
es: Urraca Cola de Serrada
ja: キリオオナガ
cn:塔尾树鹊
Temnurus temnurus

adult

Eurasian Magpie
de:Elster
fr: Pie bavarde
es: Urraca de Pico Negro
ja: カササギ
cn:喜鹊
Pica pica

www.avitopia.net/bird.en/?vid=4176801
www.avitopia.net/bird.en/?aud=4176801

adult

House Crow
de:Glanzkrähe
fr: Corbeau familier
es: Cuervo Casero
ja: イエガラス
cn:家鸦
Corvus splendens
Introduced.

adult

Large-billed Crow
de:Dschungelkrähe
fr: Corbeau à gros bec
es: Cuervo de la Selva
ja: ハシブトガラス
cn:大嘴乌鸦
Corvus macrorhynchos

adult

S3.0

Photo Meng Xianwei

Collared Crow
de:Halsbandkrähe
fr: Corbeau à collier
es: Cuervo de Collar
ja: クビワガラス
cn:白颈鸦
Corvus torquatus
Near threatened.

adult

Larks - *Alaudidae*

The family of Larks occurs all over the world with the exception of New Zealand and many islands. Larks are rather small birds (12 cm - 23 cm). In most species, the claw of the hind toe is long and pointed. They love open terrain and advance into the hottest deserts. They look for food on the ground and eat insects, snails, seeds and buds. The fluid requirement is often met from food. Some species protect their nest hollow on the windward side with a little stone wall. The chicks are looked after by both parents; the nestling period is very short.

PD

Drawing H.Groenvold

Horsfield's Bush Lark
de:Horsfieldlerche
fr: Alouette de Java
es: Alondra de Java
ja: ヤブヒバリ
cn:歌百灵
Mirafra javanica

♂ adult

S2.0

Photo Francesco Veronesi

Indochinese Bush Lark
de:Indochinalerche
fr: Alouette d'Indochine
es: Alondra Indochina
ja: ズアカヤブヒバリ
cn:印度支那歌百灵
Mirafra erythrocephala

adult

Oriental Skylark
de:Kleine Feldlerche
fr: Alouette gulgule
es: Alondra Oriental
ja: タイワンヒバリ
cn:小云雀
Alauda gulgula

adult

Swallows - *Hirundinidae*

The family of Swallows is found all over the world with the exception of the coldest regions, many species are migratory birds. They are quite small birds with a body length of 10 cm to 23 cm. The wings are long and pointed, the legs and feet small, the beak short with a wide throat. Swallows are fast and extremely agile fliers. They feed exclusively on flying insects. They nest in dug earth caves, natural caves or bowl-shaped mud nests. They breed up to three times a year.

Gray-throated Martin
de:Graukehl-Uferschwalbe
fr: Hirondelle à gorge grise
es: Avión paludícola asiático
ja: タイワンショウドウツバメ
cn:灰喉沙燕
Riparia chinensis

adult

Sand Martin
de:Uferschwalbe
fr: Hirondelle de rivage
es: Avión Zapador
ja: ショウドウツバメ
cn:崖沙燕
Riparia riparia

www.avitopia.net/bird.en/?vid=4450904
www.avitopia.net/bird.en/?aud=4450904

adult

Drawing C.W.Wyatt

adult

PD Dusky Crag Martin
de:Einfarbschwalbe
fr: Hirondelle concolore
es: Avión Oscuro
ja: インドチャイロツバメ
cn:纯色岩燕
Ptyonoprogne concolor

Photo W.J.Daunicht

adult

AU Barn Swallow
de:Rauchschwalbe
fr: Hirondelle rustique
es: Golondrina Común
ja: ツバメ
cn:家燕
Hirundo rustica

🔊 www.avitopia.net/bird.en/?kom=4451201
🎞 www.avitopia.net/bird.en/?vid=4451201

Photo W.J.Daunicht

adult

AU Wire-tailed Swallow
de:Rotkappenschwalbe
fr: Hirondelle à longs brins
es: Golondrina Colilarga
ja: ハリオツバメ
cn:线尾燕
Hirundo smithii

Photo W.J.Daunicht

adult

AU Pacific Swallow
de:Südseeschwalbe
fr: Hirondelle de Tahiti
es: Golondrina del Pacífico
ja: インドツバメ
cn:洋燕
Hirundo tahitica

Red-rumped Swallow
de:Rötelschwalbe
fr: Hirondelle rousseline
es:Golondrina Dáurica
ja: コシアカツバメ
cn:金腰燕
Cecropis daurica

AU

Photo W.J.Daunicht

adult

Striated Swallow
de:Strichelschwalbe
fr: Hirondelle striolée
es:Golondrina Estriada
ja: オオコシアカツバメ
cn:斑腰燕
Cecropis striolata

PD

Drawing C.W.Wyatt

adult

Common House Martin
de:Mehlschwalbe
fr: Hirondelle de fenêtre
es: Avión Común
ja: ニシイワツバメ
cn:毛脚燕
Delichon urbicum

🔊 www.avitopia.net/bird.en/?kom=4451501
▢ www.avitopia.net/bird.en/?vid=4451501

AU

Photo W.J.Daunicht

adult

Asian House Martin
de:Kaschmirschwalbe
fr: Hirondelle de Bonaparte
es: Avión Asiático
ja: イワツバメ
cn:烟腹毛脚燕
Delichon dasypus

PD

Drawing C.W.Wyatt

adult

PD Nepal House Martin
de:Nepalschwalbe
fr: Hirondelle du Népal
es: Avión Nepalí
ja: ノドグロイワツバメ
cn:黑喉毛脚燕
Delichon nipalense

adult

Fairy Flycatchers - *Stenostiridae*

The family of Fairy Flycatchers is found in sub-Saharan Africa and Southeast Asia. This family was recently put together on the basis of molecular biological studies. These species were previously assigned to three different families. Their body length is between 11 cm and 18 cm. Their diet consists of small insects and other invertebrates that are hunted in bushes and trees.

PD Yellow-bellied Fantail
de:Goldbauch-Fächerschwanz
fr: Rhipidure à ventre jaune
es: Cola de Abanico de Vientre Amarillo
ja: キバラオウギビタキ
cn:黄腹扇尾鹟
Chelidorhynx hypoxantha

adult

PD Grey-headed Canary-Flycatcher
de:Graukopf-Kanarienschnäpper
fr: Gobemouche à tête grise
es: Papamoscas Canario de Cabeza Gris
ja: ハイガシラヒタキ
cn:方尾鹟
Culicicapa ceylonensis

adult

Tits - *Paridae*

The family of Tits are found on all continents of the world except South America and Australia. They are small birds with a body length of 8 cm to 21 cm. Tits usually live in trees and are rather bad fliers. Some species hide food in autumn, which they bring out again in winter. Up to 14 eggs can belong to a brood and are incubated by the female alone.

Yellow-browed Tit
   de: Laubmeise
   fr: Mésange modeste
   es: Carbonero de Cejas Amarillas
   ja: キマユガラ
   cn: 黄眉林雀
Sylviparus modestus

adult

Sultan Tit
   de: Sultansmeise
   fr: Mésange sultane
   es: Carbonero Sultán
   ja: サルタンガラ
   cn: 冕雀
Melanochlora sultanea

adult

Green-backed Tit
   de: Bergkohlmeise
   fr: Mésange montagnarde
   es: Carbonero de Lomo Verde
   ja: キバラシジュウカラ
   cn: 绿背山雀
Parus monticolus

adult

Photo Lip Kee Yap

S2.0

adult

Cinereous Tit
de:Indienmeise
fr: Mésange indienne
es:Carbonero Indio
ja: クロシジュウカラ
cn:苍背山雀
Parus cinereus

Photo Lip Kee Yap

S2.0

adult

Japanese Tit
de:Japanmeise
fr: Mésange de Chine
es:Carbonero Japonés
ja: シジュウカラ
cn:远东山雀
Parus minor

Drawing J.Gould&H.C.Richter

PD

♂ adult

Yellow-cheeked Tit
de:Königsmeise
fr: Mésange à dos tacheté
es:Carbonero Chino
ja: セボシカンムリガラ
cn:黄颊山雀
Machlolophus spilonotus

Long-tailed Tits - *Aegithalidae*

The family of Long-tailed Tits is found in North America and Eurasia. They are tiny to small birds with a body length of 8.5 cm to 14 cm. They have short round wings and short bills. The tail is disproportionately long. Long-tailed tits build relatively tall closed nests with a side entrance near the top. The nests are camouflaged with lichen on the outside and lined with lots of small feathers on the inside. The female alone incubates a clutch of up to 12 eggs.

Black-throated Bushtit
  de:Rotkopf-Schwanzmeise
  fr: Mésange à tête rousse
  es: Sastrecito de Cabeza Roja
  ja: ズアカエナガ
  cn:红头长尾山雀
Aegithalos concinnus

adult

Nuthatches - *Sittidae*

The family of Nuthatches occurs in North America and Eurasia. They are rather small birds with a body length of 10.5 cm to 19.5 cm. The wings are long, the tail and legs are short, and the toes are relatively long. The beak is long, straight, pointed and quite powerful. Many species have a dark streak through the eyes. Nuthatches can also walk head down. They nest in caves in trees or rocks. The entrance is often plastered with mud. Or they build clay nests with a small entrance tube.

Chestnut-bellied Nuthatch
  de:Zimtbauchkleiber
  fr: Sittelle de Blyth
  es: Trepador Ventricastaño
  ja: クリハラゴジュウカラ
  cn:栗腹䴓
Sitta cinnamoventris

♂♀ adult

156

adult

S3.0 Neglected Nuthatch
de:Burmakleiber
fr: Sitelle d'Indochine
es:Trepador Indochino
ja: ブルマゴジュウカラ
cn:缅甸鳾
Sitta neglecta

Drawing Totodu74

adult

PD Chestnut-vented Nuthatch
de:Nagakleiber
fr: Sittelle des Naga
es:Trepador de las Naga
ja: ミナミゴジュウカラ
cn:栗臀鳾
Sitta nagaensis

Drawing J.Gould&W.M.Hart

adult

PD White-tailed Nuthatch
de:Weißschwanzkleiber
fr: Sittelle de l'Himalaya
es:Sita de Cola Blanca
ja: オジロゴジュウカラ
cn:白尾鳾
Sitta himalayensis

Drawing J.Gould&H.C.Richter

adult

PD Velvet-fronted Nuthatch
de:Samtstirnkleiber
fr: Sittelle veloutée
es: Sita Frente de Terciopleo
ja: アカハシゴジュウカラ
cn:绒额鳾
Sitta frontalis

Drawing ECSB

Yellow-billed Nuthatch
  de:Gelbschnabelkleiber
  fr: Sittelle à bec jaune
  es: Sita Lilac
  ja: キバシゴジュウガラ
  cn:淡紫鳲
Sitta solangiae
Near threatened.

adult

Beautiful Nuthatch
  de:Schmuckkleiber
  fr: Sittelle superbe
  es: Sita Preciosa
  ja: ビナンゴジュウガラ
  cn:丽鳲
Sitta formosa
Vulnerable.

adult

Holarctic Treecreepers - *Certhiidae*

The family of Treecreepers occurs in North America, Eurasia, and Africa. The small birds (11 cm - 15 cm) have short wings, a long, slender and curved beak and very large feet with long claws. They use the short stiff tail as a support when climbing. They climb the trunks with jerky movements and fly from above to the base of the next tree. Their diet consists entirely of insects. The nest is built from natural materials as a bowl in a gap or behind protruding bark.

Manipur Treecreeper
  de:Manipurbaumläufer
  fr: Grimpereau de Manipur
  es: Trepador de Manipur
  ja: マニプルキバシリ
  cn:休氏旋木雀
Certhia manipurensis

adult

Dippers - *Cinclidae*

The family od Dippers is found in America and Eurasia. The birds are clumsy with short wings and a short tail that is frequently cocked. The body length ranges from 14 cm to 23 cm. They have dense plumage and are well adapted to their habitat, fast-flowing mountain streams. They use their wings to swim underwater and can also walk on the bottom of the stream. They feed on invertebrates. The spherical nest is created in caves, often under a waterfall.

S3.0

Photo M.Nishimura

Brown Dipper
de: Flusswasseramsel
fr: Cincle de Pallas
es: Mirlo Acuático Castaño
ja: カワガラス
cn: 褐河乌
Cinclus pallasii

adult

Bulbuls - *Pycnonotidae*

The family of Bulbuls is widespread in Africa including Madagascar and in South Asia. The northern species are migratory birds. The body length ranges from 15 cm to 30 cm. They have short wings and many species have a feather crest. The Bulbuls are rather poor fliers, but move around the branches quite skillfully. Their diet is mainly vegetable, but they also eat insects. The bowl-shaped nest is built from plant material deep in the bushes. The altricial nestlings are looked after by both parents.

PD

Drawing J.Gould&H.C.Richter

Crested Finchbill
de: Finkenbülbül
fr: Bulbul à gros bec
es: Pico de Pinzón Copetón
ja: カンムリカヤノボリ
cn: 凤头雀嘴鹎
Spizixos canifrons

♂ adult

Collared Finchbill
  de: Halsbandbülbül
  fr: Bulbul à semi-collier
  es: Pico de Pinzón Acollarado
  ja: カヤノボリ
  cn: 领雀嘴鹎
Spizixos semitorques

♂ adult

Black-headed Bulbul
  de: Schwarzkopfbülbül
  fr: Bulbul cap-nègre
  es: Bulbul de Cabeza Negra
  ja: ズグロヒヨドリ
  cn: 黑头鹎
Pycnonotus atriceps

adult

Striated Bulbul
  de: Streifenbülbül
  fr: Bulbul strié
  es: Bulbul Estriado Verde
  ja: タテフヒヨドリ
  cn: 纵纹绿鹎
Pycnonotus striatus

adult

Black-crested Bulbul
  de: Goldbrustbülbül
  fr: Bulbul à huppe noire
  es: Bulbul crestinegro
  ja: クロボウシヒヨドリ
  cn: 黑冠鹎
Pycnonotus flaviventris

adult

Photo W.J.Daunicht

adult

Red-whiskered Bulbul
de:Rotohrbülbül
fr: Bulbul orphée
es: Bulbul de Bigotes Rojos
ja: コウラウン
cn:红耳鹎

Pycnonotus jocosus

AU

🔊 www.avitopia.net/bird.en/?kom=4726620
🎞 www.avitopia.net/bird.en/?vid=4726620

Drawing J.G.Keulemans

adult

Brown-breasted Bulbul
de:Braunbrustbülbül
fr: Bulbul à poitrine brune
es: Bulbul de Anderson
ja: ノドジロヒヨドリ
cn:黄臀鹎

Pycnonotus xanthorrhous

PD

Photo W.J.Daunicht

adult

Light-vented Bulbul
de:Chinabülbül
fr: Bulbul de Chine
es: Bulbul Chino
ja: シロガシラ
cn:白头鹎

Pycnonotus sinensis

AU

Photo Doug Janson

adult

Sooty-headed Bulbul
de:Kotilangbülbül
fr: Bulbul cul-d'or
es: Bulbul de Cabeza Oscura
ja: コシジロヒヨドリ
cn:白喉红臀鹎

Pycnonotus aurigaster

S3.0

Stripe-throated Bulbul
 de:Streifenkehlbülbül
 fr: Bulbul de Finlayson
 es: Bulbul de Garganta Rayada
 ja: キビタイヒヨドリ
 cn: 纹喉鹎
Pycnonotus finlaysoni

adult

Flavescent Bulbul
 de:Gelbwangenbülbül
 fr: Bulbul flavescent
 es: Bulbul Amarillento
 ja: カオジロヒヨドリ
 cn: 黄绿鹎
Pycnonotus flavescens

adult

Yellow-vented Bulbul
 de:Augenstreifbülbül
 fr: Bulbul goiavier
 es: Bulbul de Cola Amarilla
 ja: メグロヒヨドリ
 cn: 白眉黄臀鹎
Pycnonotus goiavier

adult

Streak-eared Bulbul
 de:Conradbülbül
 fr: Bulbul de Conrad
 es: Bulbul de Cachetes Rayados
 ja: ミミスジヒヨドリ
 cn: 条耳鹎
Pycnonotus conradi

adult

adult

Drawing Gossipguy

S3.0

Bare-faced Bulbul
de:Kahlkopfbülbül
fr: Bulbul hualon
es: Bulbul Caripelado
ja: ハゲガオヒヨドリ
cn:睁眼鹎
Pycnonotus hualon

adult

Photo Lip Kee

S2.0

Puff-throated Bulbul
de:Blassbauchbülbül
fr: Bulbul pâle
es: Bulbul Barbudo Olivo
ja: ノドジロカンムリヒヨドリ
cn:白喉冠鹎
Alophoixus pallidus

adult

Drawing H.Groenvold

PD

Ochraceous Bulbul
de:Rostbauchbülbül
fr: Bulbul ocré
es: Bulbul Barbudo Ocre
ja: シロハラカンムリヒヨドリ
cn:白喉褐冠鹎
Alophoixus ochraceus

adult

Photo JJ Harrison

S3.0

Grey-eyed Bulbul
de:Grauaugenbülbül
fr: Bulbul aux yeux gris
es: Bulbul de Ojos Grises
ja: メジロヒヨドリ
cn:灰眼短脚鹎
Iole propinqua

Black Bulbul
  de:China-Rotschnabelbülbül
  fr: Bulbul noir
  es: Bulbul Negro
  ja: クロヒヨドリ
  cn:黑短脚鹎
Hypsipetes leucocephalus

adult

Ashy Bulbul
  de:Braunohrbülbül
  fr: Bulbul à ailes vertes
  es: Bulbul Ahumado
  ja: キバネヒヨドリ
  cn:灰短脚鹎
Hemixos flavala

adult

Chestnut Bulbul
  de:Kastanienbülbül
  fr: Bulbul marron
  es: Bulbul Marrón
  ja: クリイロヒヨドリ
  cn:栗背短脚鹎
Hemixos castanonotus

adult

Mountain Bulbul
  de:Grünflügelbülbül
  fr: Bulbul de McClelland
  es: Bulbul Montañés
  ja: ニコバルヒヨドリ
  cn:绿翅短脚鹎
Ixos mcclellandii

adult

Cupwings - *Pnoepygidae*

The family of Cupwings or Wren-babblers have only recently been separated from the former extensive family of the Timalias and elevated to family rank due to DNA tests. They occur exclusively in the oriental region. They are tiny birds with a body length of 7.5 cm to 10 cm. They have an extremely reduced, usually invisible tail. They are usually close to the ground between dense undergrowth. They mainly live on insects and small arthropods. The nest is spherical with an entrance on the top.

adult

Photo J.M.Garg

S3.0

Scaly-breasted Wren-Babbler
  de:Schuppentimalie
  fr: Turdinule à ventre blanc
  es:Charlatán-Troglodita de Pecho Escamoso
  ja:ヒメサザイチメドリ
  cn:鳞胸鹪鹛
Pnoepyga albiventer

adult

Photo Dibyendu Ash

S3.0

Pygmy Wren-Babbler
  de:Moosschuppentimalie
  fr: Turdinule maillée
  es:Charlatán-Troglodita Pigmeo
  ja:タカサゴミソサザイ
  cn:小鳞胸鹪鹛
Pnoepyga pusilla

Bush-Warblers and allies - *Scotocercidae*

The family of Bush-warblers and allies occurs in Africa, Eurasia and some islands in the Pacific. The family was recently separated from the family of Old World Warblers based on DNA testing. They are small birds between 7 cm and 15 cm in length. Some species have very short tails. The plumage shows no bright colors.

Pale-footed Bush Warbler
  de: Weißfuß-Buschsänger
  fr: Bouscarle à pattes claires
  es: Ruiseñor Bastardo de Patas Pálidas
  ja: キアシヤブサメ
  cn: 淡脚树莺
Urosphena pallidipes

adult

Asian Stubtail
  de: Stummelsänger
  fr: Bouscarle de Swinhoe
  es: Colirobusto de Cabeza Escamosa
  ja: ヤブサメ
  cn: 鳞头树莺
Urosphena squameiceps

adult

Grey-bellied Tesia
  de: Olivscheiteltesia
  fr: Tésie à sourcils jaunes
  es: Trinador de Vientre Gris
  ja: キマユコビトサザイ
  cn: 灰腹地莺
Tesia cyaniventer

adult

Drawing J.G.Keulemans

Drawing J.Smit

Drawing J.Gould&H.C.Richter

adult

Drawing Brian Small

A2.0 Slaty-bellied Tesia
de:Goldscheiteltesia
fr: Tésie à ventre ardoise
es:Trinador de Vientre Pizarro
ja: クロハラコビトサザイ
cn:金冠地莺
Tesia olivea

adult

Drawing J.Gould&H.C.Richter

PD Chestnut-headed Tesia
de:Rotkopftesia
fr: Tésie à tête marron
es:Trinador de Cabeza Castaña
ja: クリガシラコビトサザイ
cn:栗头地莺
Cettia castaneocoronata

adult

Drawing J.G.Keulemans

PD Yellow-bellied Warbler
de:Bambuslaubsänger
fr: Pouillot à sourcils blancs
es:Mosquitero de Cejas Blancas
ja: マミジロムシクイ
cn:黄腹鹛莺
Abroscopus superciliaris

adult

Drawing Jan Wilczur

A2.0 Rufous-faced Warbler
de:Rostwangen-Laubsänger
fr: Pouillot à gorge blanche
es:Mosquitero de Cara Rufa
ja: コシジロムシクイ
cn:棕脸鹛莺
Abroscopus albogularis

adult

Black-faced Warbler
de:Schieferkopf-Laubsänger
fr: Pouillot à face noire
es: Mosquitero de Cara Negra
ja: カオグロムシクイ
cn:黑脸鹟莺
Abroscopus schisticeps

adult

Mountain Tailorbird
de:Bergschneidervogel
fr: Couturière montagnarde
es: Sastrecillo Montano
ja: キバラサイホウチョウ
cn:栗头缝叶莺
Phyllergates cucullatus

adult

Broad-billed Warbler
de:Breitschnabel-Laubsänger
fr: Pouillot de Hodgson
es: Mosquitero de Pico Ancho
ja: ズアカムシクイ
cn:宽嘴鹟莺
Tickellia hodgsoni

adult

Japanese Bush Warbler
de:Japanbuschsänger
fr: Bouscarle chanteuse
es: Ruiseñor Bastardo Japonés
ja: ウグイス
cn:日本树莺
Horornis diphone

adult

adult

Photo J.M.Garg

A3.0

Brown-flanked Bush Warbler
de:Bergbuschsänger
fr: Bouscarle de montagne
es:Ruiseñor Bastardo de Patas Fuerte
ja: タイワンコウグイス
cn:强脚树莺
Horornis fortipes

adult

A2.0

Aberrant Bush Warbler
de:Olivbuschsänger
fr: Bouscarle jaune et vert
es:Ruiseñor Bastardo Aberrante
ja: キバラウグイス
cn:异色树莺
Horornis flavolivaceus

Drawing Brian Small

Leaf Warblers - *Phylloscopidae*

The warbler family of Leaf-warblers occurs in Eurasia and Africa and only one species reaches America, Alaska, but many species are long-distance migrants. With 9 cm to 14 cm, they are rather small birds that are predominantly greenish or brownish in color. They live in dense vegetation and feed on insects. The nests are created at a low height, are closed and have a side entrance.

♂ adult

Drawing J.G.Keulemans

PD

Dusky Warbler
de:Dunkellaubsänger
fr: Pouillot brun
es:Mosquitero Sombrío
ja: ムジセッカ
cn:褐柳莺
Phylloscopus fuscatus

Buff-throated Warbler

de:Dornlaubsänger
fr: Pouillot subaffin
es: Mosquitero de Garganta Crema
ja: バフイロムシクイ
cn:棕腹柳莺
Phylloscopus subaffinis

adult

Photo Ron Knight

Yellow-streaked Warbler

de:Davidlaubsänger
fr: Pouillot de Milne-Edwards
es: Mosquitero de Milne-Edwards
ja: モウコムジセッカ
cn:棕眉柳莺
Phylloscopus armandii

adult

Drawing Huet

Radde's Warbler

de:Bartlaubsänger
fr: Pouillot de Schwarz
es: Mosquitero de Schwarz
ja: カラフトムジセッカ
cn:巨嘴柳莺
Phylloscopus schwarzi

adult

Drawing J.G.Keulemans

Buff-barred Warbler

de:Goldbinden-Laubsänger
fr: Pouillot élégant
es: Mosquitero de Barras Anaranjadas
ja: アカバネムシクイ
cn:橙斑翅柳莺
Phylloscopus pulcher

adult

Photo Jason Thompson

adult

Ashy-throated Warbler
de:Graukehl-Laubsänger
fr: Pouillot à face grise
es: Mosquitero de Cara Gris
ja: キゴシムシクイ
cn:灰喉柳莺
Phylloscopus maculipennis

S3.0

adult

Pallas's Leaf Warbler
de:Goldhähnchen-Laubsänger
fr: Pouillot de Pallas
es: Mosquitero de Pallas
ja: カラフトムシクイ
cn:黄腰柳莺
Phylloscopus proregulus

PD

Drawing J.G.Keulemans

adult

Sichuan Leaf Warbler
de:Sichuanlaubsänger
fr: Pouillot de Lichiang
es: Mosquitero de Forrest
ja: シセンムシクイ
cn:四川柳莺
Phylloscopus forresti

AU

Drawing W.J.Daunicht

adult

Chinese Leaf Warbler
de:Yunnanlaubsänger
fr: Pouillot du Sitchouan
es: Mosquitero de Sichuán
ja: シセンムシクイ
cn:四川柳莺
Phylloscopus yunnanensis

A2.0

Photo Ron Knight

Photo Umeshsrinivasan

Yellow-browed Warbler
de:Gelbbrauen-Laubsänger
fr: Pouillot à grands sourcils
es: Mosquitero Bilistado
ja: キマユムシクイ
cn: 黄眉柳莺
Phylloscopus inornatus

adult

Photo W.J.Daunicht

AU

Hume's Leaf Warbler
de:Tienschanlaubsänger
fr: Pouillot de Hume
es: Mosquitero de Hume
ja: バフマユムシクイ
cn: 淡眉柳莺
Phylloscopus humei

adult

Drawing J.G.Keulemans

PD

Arctic Warbler
de:Wanderlaubsänger
fr: Pouillot boréal
es: Mosquitero Boreal
ja: メボソムシクイ
cn: 极北柳莺
Phylloscopus borealis

adult

Photo Alnus

S3.0

Kamchatka Leaf Warbler
de:Kamtschatkalaubsänger
fr: Pouillot du Kamtchatka
es: Mosquitero de Kamchatka
ja: オオムシクイ
cn: 堪察加柳莺
Phylloscopus examinandus

adult

Drawing W.J.Daunicht

AU

adult

Photo W.D.G.Daunicht

LIC

Greenish Warbler
de:Grünlaubsänger
fr: Pouillot verdâtre
es:Mosquitero Troquiloide
ja:ヤナギムシクイ
cn:暗绿柳莺
Phylloscopus trochiloides

♂ adult

Drawing G.Muetzel

PD

Two-barred Warbler
de:Middendorfflaubsänger
fr: Pouillot à deux barres
es:Mosquitero de dos Barras
ja:フタオビヤナギムシクイ
cn:双斑绿柳莺
Phylloscopus plumbeitarsus

♂ adult

Drawing G.Muetzel

PD

Pale-legged Leaf Warbler
de:Ussurilaubsänger
fr: Pouillot à pattes claires
es:Mosquitero de Patas Pálidas
ja:エゾムシクイ
cn:淡脚柳莺
Phylloscopus tenellipes

adult

Photo Gin tonic

PD

Sakhalin Leaf Warbler
de:Portenkolaubsänger
fr: Pouillot du Japon
es:Mosquitero borealoide
ja:エゾムシクイ
cn:日本淡脚柳莺
Phylloscopus borealoides

173

Eastern Crowned Warbler
de:Kronenlaubsänger
fr: Pouillot de Temminck
es:Mosquitero de Temminck
ja:センダイムシクイ
cn:冕柳莺
Phylloscopus coronatus

♂ adult

Blyth's Leaf Warbler
de:Streifenkopf-Laubsänger
fr: Pouillot de Blyth
es:Mosquitero de Blyth
ja:ヒマラヤムシクイ
cn:冠纹柳莺
Phylloscopus reguloides

adult

Claudia's Leaf Warbler
de:Claudialaubsänger
fr: Pouillot de Claudia
es:Mosquitero de Claudia
ja:クラウディアムシクイ
cn:冠纹柳莺
Phylloscopus claudiae

adult

White-tailed Leaf Warbler
de:Weißschwanz-Laubsänger
fr: Pouillot de Davison
es:Mosquitero de Cola Blanca
ja:オジロムシクイ
cn:云南白斑尾柳莺
Phylloscopus davisoni

adult

adult

Photo Ron Knight

A2.0

Kloss's Leaf Warbler
    de:Ogilvielaubsänger
    fr: Pouillot d'Ogilvie-Grant
    es:Mosquitero de Davison
    ja: オジロムシクイ
    cn:白斑尾柳莺
    Phylloscopus ogilviegranti

adult

Drawing L.Shyamal

S3.0

Limestone Leaf Warbler
    de:Karstlaubsänger
    fr: Pouillot calciatile
    es:Mosquitero Roquero
    ja:セッカイガンムシクイ
    cn:灰岩柳莺
    Phylloscopus calciatilis

adult

Photo Pkspks

PD

Yellow-vented Warbler
    de:Gelbbrust-Laubsänger
    fr: Pouillot chanteur
    es:Mosquitero de Cara Amarilla
    ja: キムネムシクイ
    cn:黄胸柳莺
    Phylloscopus cantator

adult

Drawing J.G.Keulemans

PD

Sulphur-breasted Warbler
    de:Goldscheitel-Laubsänger
    fr: Pouillot de Rickett
    es:Mosquitero de Cejas Negras
    ja: マユグロムシクイ
    cn:黑眉柳莺
    Phylloscopus ricketti

Grey-crowned Warbler

de:Grauscheitel-Laubsänger
fr: Pouillot à calotte grise
es: Mosquitero de Corona Gris
ja: ハイガシラモリムシクイ
cn:灰冠鹟莺

Seicercus tephrocephalus

adult

Drawing J.G.Keulemans

PD

Plain-tailed Warbler

de:Einfarbschwanz-Laubsänger
fr: Pouillot à queue unie
es: Mosquitero de Cola Descolorida
ja: ムジオモリムシクイ
cn:淡尾鹟莺

Seicercus soror

adult

Drawing W.J.Daunicht

AU

Omei Warbler

de:Omeilaubsänger
fr: Pouillot de Taibai
es: Mosquitero de Martens
ja: ガビモリムシクイ
cn:峨嵋鹟莺

Seicercus omeiensis

adult

Drawing W.J.Daunicht

AU

Bianchi's Warbler

de:Bianchi-Brillenlaubsänger
fr: Pouillot de Bianchi
es: Mosquitero de Bianchi
ja: ビアンキモリムシクイ
cn:比氏鹟莺

Seicercus valentini

adult

Photo Yu Yat Tung

S4.0

adult

Photo Dibyendu Ash

S3.0

White-spectacled Warbler
de:Silberbrillen-Laubsänger
fr: Pouillot affin
es:Mosquitero de Ojos Blancos
ja: メジロモリムシクイ
cn:白眶鶲莺
Seicercus affinis

adult

Photo Dibyendu Ash

S3.0

Grey-cheeked Warbler
de:Grauwangen-Laubsänger
fr: Pouillot à joues grises
es:Mosquitero de Mejillas Grises
ja: アゴジロモリムシクイ
cn:灰脸鶲莺
Seicercus poliogenys

adult

Photo Dibyendu Ash

S3.0

Chestnut-crowned Warbler
de:Rotkopf-Laubsänger
fr: Pouillot à couronne marron
es:Mosquitero Coronicastaño
ja: クリガシラモリムシクイ
cn:栗头鶲莺
Seicercus castaniceps

Reed-Warblers and allies - *Acrocephalidae*

The family of Reed-Warblers is native to Africa, Eurasia and Australia to Oceania. Many species are migratory birds. This family was only recently recognized based on DNA studies. The body size ranges from 11.5 cm to 18 cm. Almost all species have a relatively single-coloured plumage and can be better identified from their songs than from their appearance. However, the chants often contain imitations of other bird species. Most Reed-Warblers colonize wetlands or habitats near water.

Thick-billed Warbler
de: Dickschnabel-Rohrsänger
fr: Rousserolle à gros bec
es: Carricero de Pico Grueso
ja: ハシブトオオヨシキリ
cn: 厚嘴苇莺
Iduna aedon

adult

Black-browed Reed Warbler
de: Brauenrohrsänger
fr: Rousserolle de Schrenck
es: Carricerín de Schrenk
ja: コヨシキリ
cn: 黑眉苇莺
Acrocephalus bistrigiceps

♂ adult

Blunt-winged Warbler
de: Strauchrohrsänger
fr: Rousserolle de Swinhoe
es: Carricero de Alas Abruptas
ja: コバネヨシキリ
cn: 钝翅苇莺
Acrocephalus concinens

adult

adult

AU **Manchurian Reed Warbler**
de:Mandschurenrohrsänger
fr: Rousserolle mandchoue
es: Carricero Manchú
ja: コクリュウコウインダヨシキリ
cn:远东苇莺
Acrocephalus tangorum
Vulnerable.

adult

PD **Oriental Reed Warbler**
de:Chinarohrsänger
fr: Rousserolle d'Orient
es: Carricero Oriental
ja: オオヨシキリ
cn:东方大苇莺
Acrocephalus orientalis

adult

S2.0 **Clamorous Reed Warbler**
de:Stentorrohrsänger
fr: Rousserolle stentor
es: Carricero Aclamador
ja: チュウヨシキリ
cn:噪大苇莺
Acrocephalus stentoreus

Grassbirds and allies - *Locustellidae*

The family of grassbirds is common in Africa, Eurasia, and Australia. This family was only recently recognized on the basis of DNA studies. They are small, slender birds, the long tail is rounded and graduated. Grass warblers live in a wide variety of habitats, from grasslands to forests.

Striated Grassbird
de:Strichelkopf-Schilfsteiger
fr: Mégalure des marais
es: Yerbera de Cabeza Estriada
ja: オニセッカ
cn:沼泽大尾莺
Megalurus palustris

Pallas's Grasshopper Warbler
de:Streifenschwirl
fr: Locustelle de Pallas
es: Buscarla de Pallas
ja: シベリアセンニュウ
cn:小蝗莺
Locustella certhiola

Pleske's Grasshopper Warbler
de:Pleskeschwirl
fr: Locustelle de Pleske
es: Buscarla de Styan
ja: ウチヤマセンニュウ
cn:史氏蝗莺
Locustella pleskei
Vulnerable.

adult

adult

adult

Drawing Pretre

Drawing J.G.Keulemans

Drawing W.J.Daunicht

PD

PD

AU

adult

Photo Tim Loseby

S4.0

Lanceolated Warbler
de:Strichelschwirl
fr: Locustelle lancéolée
es: Buscarla Lanceolada
ja: マキノセンニュウ
cn:矛斑蝗莺
Locustella lanceolata

♀ adult

Drawing G.Muetzel

PD

Brown Bush Warbler
de:Rostbuschsänger
fr: Bouscarle russule
es: Zarzalero Pardo
ja: チャイロオウギセッカ
cn:棕褐短翅莺
Locustella luteoventris

adult

Drawing W.J.Daunicht

AU

Chinese Bush-Warbler
de:Taczanowskibuschsänger
fr: Bouscarle de Taczanowski
es: Zarzalero de Taczanowski
ja: シベリアオウギセッカ
cn:中华短翅莺
Locustella tacsanowskia

adult

Photo Mike Prince

A2.0

Baikal Bush Warbler
de:Davidbuschsänger
fr: Bouscarle de David
es: Zarzalero de David
ja: シベリアムナフオウギセッカ
cn:北短翅莺
Locustella davidi

Russet Bush Warbler
de:Mandellbuschsänger
fr: Bouscarle de Mandell
es: Zarzalero de Mandell
ja: タイワンオオセッカ
cn:黄褐短翅莺
Locustella mandelli

adult

Cisticolas and allies - *Cisticolidae*

The family of Cisticolas and allies occurs in the Old World, but is confined to temperate and warm areas. This family was recently separated from the earlier extensive family of Old World Warblers and reorganized based on DNA studies. They are small birds between 9 cm and 20 cm in length. Many of the species have long and graduated tails. They live on small invertebrates. The nests are made with a lot of effort, some species, the tailor birds, literally sew large leaves together to give the nest a cover.

Zitting Cisticola
de:Cistensänger
fr: Cisticole des joncs
es: Buitrón Común
ja: セッカ
cn:棕扇尾莺
Cisticola juncidis

adult

Golden-headed Cisticola
de:Goldkopf-Cistensänger
fr: Cisticole à couronne dorée
es: Buitrón de Capa Dorada
ja: タイワンセッカ
cn:金头扇尾莺
Cisticola exilis

adult

♂ adult

PD Common Tailorbird
de:Rotstirn-Schneidervogel
fr: Couturière à longue queue
es:Sastrecillo Común
ja: オナガサイホウチョウ
cn:长尾缝叶莺
Orthotomus sutorius

Drawing J.Gould&H.C.Richter

adult

PD Dark-necked Tailorbird
de:Strichelschneidervogel
fr: Couturière à col noir
es:Sastrecillo de Collar negro
ja: ノドグロサイホウチョウ
cn:黑喉缝叶莺
Orthotomus atrogularis

Drawing G.A.Levett-Yeats

adult

PD Cambodian Tailorbird
de:Kambodschaschneidervogel
fr: Couturière du Cambodge
es:Sastrecillo de Camboya
ja: カンボジアサイホウチョウ
cn:柬埔寨缝叶莺
Orthotomus chaktomuk
Near threatened.

Photo James Eaton

adult

PD Brown Prinia
de:Malaienprinie
fr: Prinia des montagnes
es:Prinia Montañés Castaña
ja: ヤマハウチワドリ
cn:褐山鹪莺
Prinia polychroa

Drawing Pretre

Hill Prinia
de:Grauwangenprinie
fr: Prinia à sourcils
es: Prinia montana
ja: マユハウチワドリ
cn:黑喉山鹪莺
Prinia superciliaris

adept
Drawing J.G.Keulemans

PD

adult

Rufescent Prinia
de:Rostprinie
fr: Prinia roussâtre
es: Prinia Cataña Pequeña
ja: チャイロハウチワドリ
cn:暗冕山鹪莺
Prinia rufescens

A2.0

Photo Ron Knight

adult

Grey-breasted Prinia
de:Graubrustprinie
fr: Prinia de Hodgson
es: Prinia de Franklin
ja: ハイムネハウチワドリ
cn:灰胸山鹪莺
Prinia hodgsonii

A3.0

Photo J.M.Garg

adult

Yellow-bellied Prinia
de:Gelbbauchprinie
fr: Prinia à ventre jaune
es: Prinia de Vientre Amarillo
ja: アオハウチワドリ
cn:黄腹山鹪莺
Prinia flaviventris

PD

Drawing J.G.Keulemans

adult

PD Plain Prinia
  de:Braunkopfprinie
  fr: Prinia simple
  es:Prinia Descolorida
  ja:マミハウチワドリ
  cn:纯色山鹪莺
  Prinia inornata

Drawing J.G.Keulemans

adult

Parrotbills - *Paradoxornithidae*

The family of Parrotbills is only found in East Asia, usually they do not migrate. The body size is between 9 cm and 28 cm. They have strong beaks and feed on seeds, especially grass seeds. Since cuckoos often intrude as brood parasites into nests of parrotbills, these have developed mechanisms to recognize parasitic eggs and reject incubation.

PD Golden-breasted Fulvetta
  de:Goldalcippe
  fr: Alcippe à poitrine dorée
  es:Fulveta de Pecho Dorado
  ja:キンムネチメドリ
  cn:金胸雀鹛
  Lioparus chrysotis

Drawing H.Groenvold

adult

PD Yellow-eyed Babbler
  de:Goldaugentimalie
  fr: Timalie aux yeux d'or
  es:Charlatán de Ojos Dorados
  ja:キンメセンニュウチメドリ
  cn:金眼鹛雀
  Chrysomma sinense

Drawing J.G.Keulemans

adult

Indochinese Fulvetta
de: Streifenwangenalcippe
fr: Fulvetta de Danis
es: Fulveta Indochina
ja: ノドジマチメドリ
cn: 印支雀鹛
Fulvetta danisi

adult

White-browed Fulvetta
de: Weißbrauenalcippe
fr: Alcippe de Hodgson
es: Fulveta de Cejas Blancas
ja: ノドジロチメドリ
cn: 白眉雀鹛
Fulvetta vinipectus

adult

Grey-hooded Fulvetta
de: Braunkopfalcippe
fr: Fulvetta à gorge rayée
es: Fulveta Encapuchada
ja: アリサンチメドリ
cn: 褐头雀鹛
Fulvetta cinereiceps

adult

Streak-throated Fulvetta
de: Streifenkehlalcippe
fr: Fulvetta de Manipur
es: Fulveta de Manipur
ja: シマノドチメドリ
cn: 印缅褐头雀鹛
Fulvetta manipurensis

adult

Drawing J.Gould&H.C.Richter

♂♀ adult

Grey-headed Parrotbill
  de:Graukopf-Papageimeise
  fr: Paradoxornis à tête grise
  es: Picoloro de Cabeza Gris
  ja: ハイガシラダルマエナガ
  cn:灰头鸦雀
Psittiparus gularis

Drawing H.Groenvold

adult

Black-crowned Parrotbill
  de:Schwarzkappen-Papageimeise
  fr: Paradoxornis à calotte noire
  es: Picoloro Cabecinegro
  ja: ズグロダルマエナガ
  cn:黑头鸦雀
Psittiparus margaritae
Endemic.
Near threatened.

Photo Francesco Veronesi

adult

S2.0 Rufous-headed Parrotbill
  de:Baker-Papageimeise
  fr: Paradoxornis de Baker
  es: Picoloro cabecirrufo oriental
  ja: オオズアカダルマエナガ
  cn:红头鸦雀
Psittiparus bakeri

Drawing J.Gould&W.M.Hart

♂♀ adult

Spot-breasted Parrotbill
  de:Brustflecken-Papageimeise
  fr: Paradoxornis fléché
  es: Picoloro de Pecho Manchado
  ja: ミミグロダルマエナガ
  cn:点胸鸦雀
Paradoxornis guttaticollis

Lesser Rufous-headed Parrotbill
  de: Schwarzbrauen-Papageimeise
  fr: Paradoxornis à sourcils noirs
  es: Picoloro de Cabeza Roja Chico
  ja: ズアカダルマエナガ
  cn: 黑眉鸦雀
Chleuasicus atrosuperciliaris

adult

Vinous-throated Parrotbill
  de: Braunkopf-Papageimeise
  fr: Paradoxornis de Webb
  es: Picoloro de Garganta Violeta
  ja: ダルマエナガ
  cn: 棕头鸦雀
Sinosuthora webbiana

adult

Ashy-throated Parrotbill
  de: Graukehl-Papageimeise
  fr: Paradoxornis à gorge cendrée
  es: Picoloro de Garganta Ahumada
  ja: ハイノドダルマエナガ
  cn: 灰喉鸦雀
Sinosuthora alphonsiana

adult

Black-throated Parrotbill
  de: Grauohr-Papageimeise
  fr: Paradoxornis à menton noir
  es: Picoloro de Blyth
  ja: キバネダルマエナガ
  cn: 橙额鸦雀
Suthora nipalensis

♂♀ adult

PD Golden Parrotbill
  de:Goldpapageimeise
  fr: Paradoxornis de Verreaux
  es: Picoloro Dorado
  ja: キバネダルマエナガ
  cn:金色鸦雀
Suthora verreauxi

Drawing H.Groenvold

adult

PD Short-tailed Parrotbill
  de:Kurzschwanz-Papageimeise
  fr: Paradoxornis de David
  es: Picoloro de David
  ja: ノドグロダルマエナガ
  cn:短尾鸦雀
Neosuthora davidiana

Drawing J.G.Keulemans

adult

White-eyes - *Zosteropidae*

The family of White-eyes has its distribution in Africa, South Asia and Australia to Samoa in the Pacific. Many species are endemic to small islands. The body size of these petite birds is between 10 cm and 14 cm. They have short wings with only nine hand feathers. The beak is slender, the tongue is brush-tipped and can be extended far. The appearance of the different species is often extremely similar. Many species have a conspicuous ring of tiny white feathers around their eyes. They are tree inhabitants and eat insects, fruits and nectar. They pierce fruit with their beak and pull the juice out with their tongue. The nest consists of a hanging bowl on a forked branch. The breeding season is the shortest for birds at 10 days.

PD Chestnut-collared Yuhina
  de:Kastanienohryuhina
  fr: Yuhina à bandeau
  es: Yuhina Indochina
  ja: インドシナミミチメドリ
  cn:栗耳凤鹛
Yuhina torqueola

Drawing J.Gould&H.C.Richter

adult

Whiskered Yuhina
de:Gelbnackenyuhina
fr: Yuhina à cou roux
es: Yujina Bigotuda
ja: チャイロカンムリチメドリ
cn:黄颈凤鹛
Yuhina flavicollis

adult

Drawing J.Gould&H.C.Richter

PD

Stripe-throated Yuhina
de:Kehlstreifenyuhina
fr: Yuhina à gorge striée
es: Yujina de Garganta Estriada
ja: ノドフカンムリチメドリ
cn:纹喉凤鹛
Yuhina gularis

adult

Photo finlap

A2.0

White-collared Yuhina
de:Diademyuhina
fr: Yuhina à diadème
es: Yujina de Collar Blanco
ja: シロエリカンムリチメドリ
cn:白领凤鹛
Yuhina diademata

adult

Photo W.J.Daunicht

AU

Black-chinned Yuhina
de:Meisenyuhina
fr: Yuhina à menton noir
es: Yujina de Copete Negro
ja: クロアゴカンムリチメドリ
cn:黑颏凤鹛
Yuhina nigrimenta

adult

Photo fisherbray

A2.0

PD

Drawing J.Gould&H.C.Richter

adult

Chestnut-flanked White-eye
de:Rostflanken-Brillenvogel
fr: Zostérops à flancs marron
es: Ojiblanco de Dorsos Castaños
ja: チョウセンメジロ
cn:红胁绣眼鸟
Zosterops erythropleurus

PD

Drawing J.Smit

adult

Oriental White-eye
de:Gangesbrillenvogel
fr: Zostérops oriental
es: Ojiblanco Oriental
ja: ハイバラメジロ
cn:灰腹绣眼鸟
Zosterops palpebrosus

S3.0

Photo Trisha Shears

adult

Japanese White-eye
de:Japanbrillenvogel
fr: Zostérops du Japon
es: Ojiblanco Japonés
ja: メジロ
cn:暗绿绣眼鸟
Zosterops japonicus

Babblers - *Timaliidae*

Several families have been separated from the former large family of the Old World Babblers, so that the range of the reduced family is now limited to Asia from Pakistan to the Philippines. They have a weak flight and are not strongly migratory. Old World Babblers are small to medium-sized forest inhabitants. They feed primarily on insects and other invertebrates, some species also eat plant-based foods when insects are scarce. The nest is usually built close to the ground from plant parts. The birds are monogamous and both parents take part in the brood care.

Chestnut-capped Babbler
de:Rotkäppchentimalie
fr: Timalie coiffée
es:Charlatán de Coronilla Castaña
ja: アカガシラチメドリ
cn:红顶鹛
Timalia pileata

adult

Photo W.J.Daunicht

AU

Striped Tit-Babbler
de:Gelbbrusttimalie
fr: Timalie à gorge striée
es:Charlatán-Paro Rayado
ja: ムナフムシクイチメドリ
cn:纹胸鹛
Mixornis gularis

adult

Drawing Pretre

PD

Grey-faced Tit-Babbler
de:Kelleytimalie
fr: Timalie de Kelley
es:Charlatán-Paro de Kelley
ja: アンナンムシクイチメドリ
cn:灰脸纹胸鹛
Mixornis kelleyi

adult

Drawing W.J.Daunicht

AU

S3.0

Photo Dibyendu Ash

adult

Golden Babbler
de:Goldkopftimalie
fr: Timalie dorée
es:Charlatán Dorado
ja: キガシラモリチメドリ
cn:金头穗鹛
Cyanoderma chrysaeum

PD

Drawing J.Gould&H.C.Richter

adult

Rufous-capped Babbler
de:Rotkopftimalie
fr: Timalie de Blyth
es:Charlatán de Coronilla Roja
ja: ズアカチメドリ
cn:红头穗鹛
Cyanoderma ruficeps

S4.0

Photo Pkspks

adult

Buff-chested Babbler
de:Haringtontimalie
fr: Timalie ambiguë
es:Charlatán de Pecho Anteado
ja: キノドズアカチメドリ
cn:黄喉穗鹛
Cyanoderma ambiguum

PD

Drawing J.Smit

adult

Rufous-fronted Babbler
de:Rotstirntimalie
fr: Timalie à front roux
es:Charlatán de Frente Rojiza
ja: ノドフズアカチメドリ
cn:红额穗鹛
Cyanoderma rufifrons

Pale-throated Wren-babbler
de: Blasskehl-Zaunkönigstimalie
fr: Timalie de Kinnear
es: Ratina Gorjipálida
ja: ノドジロオナガサザイチメドリ
cn: 淡喉鹩鹛
Spelaeornis kinneari
Vulnerable.

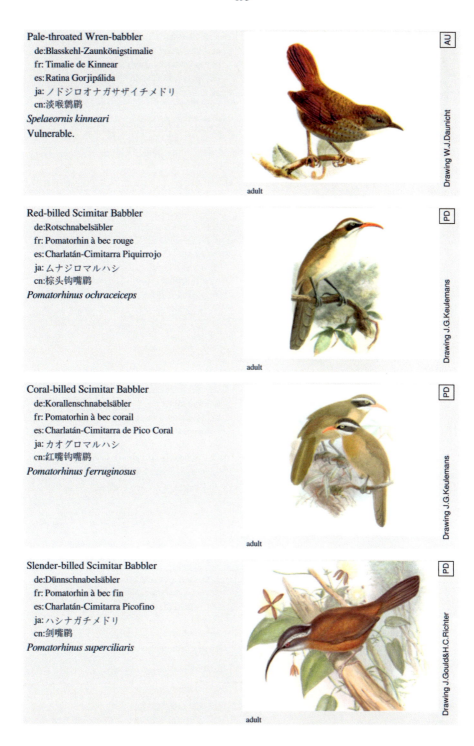

AU

Drawing W.J.Daunicht

adult

Red-billed Scimitar Babbler
de: Rotschnabelsäbler
fr: Pomatorhin à bec rouge
es: Charlatán-Cimitarra Piquirrojo
ja: ムナジロマルハシ
cn: 棕头钩嘴鹛
Pomatorhinus ochraceiceps

PD

Drawing J.G.Keulemans

adult

Coral-billed Scimitar Babbler
de: Korallenschnabelsäbler
fr: Pomatorhin à bec corail
es: Charlatán-Cimitarra de Pico Coral
ja: カオグロマルハシ
cn: 红嘴钩嘴鹛
Pomatorhinus ferruginosus

PD

Drawing J.G.Keulemans

adult

Slender-billed Scimitar Babbler
de: Dünnschnabelsäbler
fr: Pomatorhin à bec fin
es: Charlatán-Cimitarra Picofino
ja: ハシナガチメドリ
cn: 剑嘴鹛
Pomatorhinus superciliaris

PD

Drawing J.Gould&H.C.Richter

adult

adult

S2.0

Photo wagtail

Streak-breasted Scimitar-babbler
  de:Rothalssäbler
  fr: Pomatorhin à col roux
  es:Cimitarra Cuellirrufa
  ja: ヒメマルハシ
  cn:棕颈钩嘴鹛
Pomatorhinus ruficollis

♂♀ adult

PD

Drawing J.G.Keulemans

White-browed Scimitar Babbler
  de:Himalayasäbler
  fr: Pomatorhin à tête ardoise
  es:Charlatán-Cimitarra de Cabeza Pizarra
  ja: マミジロマルハシ
  cn:灰头钩嘴鹛
Pomatorhinus schisticeps

adult

PD

Drawing D.W.Mitchell

Large Scimitar Babbler
  de:Riesensäbler
  fr: Pomatorhin à long bec
  es:Charlatán-Cimitarra Piquilargo
  ja: オオマルハシ
  cn:长嘴钩嘴鹛
Megapomatorhinus hypoleucos

adult

PD

Drawing J.G.Keulemans

Black-streaked Scimitar-babbler
  de:Schwarzstrichelsäbler
  fr: Pomatorhin chanteur
  es:Cimitarra Rayada
  ja: クロスジマルハシ
  cn:斑胸钩嘴鹛
Megapomatorhinus gravivox

adult

Grey-throated Babbler
  de:Graukehl-Buschtimalie
  fr: Timalie à tête rayée
  es: Charlatán de Garganta Gris
  ja: ハイノドモリチメドリ
  cn: 黑头穗鹛
Stachyris nigriceps

adult

Spot-necked Babbler
  de: Fleckenhals-Buschtimalie
  fr: Timalie à cou tacheté
  es: Timalí Gorjipinto
  ja: エリボシモリチメドリ
  cn: 斑颈穗鹛
Stachyris strialata

adult

Sooty Babbler
  de: Laosbuschtimalie
  fr: Timalie de Herbert
  es: Charlatán Tiznado
  ja: ラオスモリチメドリ
  cn: 乌穗鹛
Stachyris herberti

adult

Nonggang Babbler
  de: Nonggangbuschtimalie
  fr: Timalie de Nonggang
  es: Timalí de Nonggang
  ja: ナンガンモリチメドリ
  cn: 弄岗穗鹛
Stachyris nonggangensis
Vulnerable.

adult

Jungle-Babblers - *Pellorneidae*

The family of Jungle-babblers lives in the rainforest belt of tropical Africa and in Southeast Asia from India to Sulawesi. The body length is 10 cm to 26 cm. Their normal habitat are forests with dense undergrowth. They mainly eat insects, spiders, snails and worms. Some species also consume berries and seeds.

adult

PD Scaly-crowned Babbler
  de:Rotstirn-Zweigtimalie
  fr: Akalat à calotte maillée
  es:Charlatán Arboreal de Corona Escamosa
  ja:コズアカチャイロチメドリ
  cn:小红头树鹛
  Malacopteron cinereum

Drawing H.Groenvold

♂♀ adult

PD Collared Babbler
  de:Brustbandtimalie
  fr: Gampsorin à collier
  es:Timalí Acollarado
  ja:エリモズチメドリ
  cn:领鹛鹛
  Gampsorhynchus torquatus

Drawing H.Groenvold

adult

S3.0 Yellow-throated Fulvetta
  de:Gelbkehlalcippe
  fr: Alcippe à gorge jaune
  es:Fulveta de Garganta Amarilla
  ja:キノドチメドリ
  cn:黄喉雀鹛
  Schoeniparus cinereus

Photo Umeshsrinivasan

Rufous-winged Fulvetta
de:Kastanienalcippe
fr: Alcippe à tête marron
es:Fulveta de Cabeza Castaña
ja: クリボウシチメドリ
cn:栗头雀鹛
Schoeniparus castaneceps

adult

Drawing J.G.Keulemans

PD

Black-crowned Fulvetta
de:Langbianalcippe
fr: Pseudominla de Kloss
es: Fulveta Coroninegra
ja: クロガシラチメドリ
cn:黑顶雀鹛
Schoeniparus klossi
Endemic.

adult

Drawing H.Groenvold

PD

Rufous-throated Fulvetta
de:Kropfbandalcippe
fr: Alcippe à gorge rousse
es:Fulveta de Garganta Rufa
ja: クビワチメドリ
cn:棕喉雀鹛
Schoeniparus rufogularis

adult

Drawing W.J.Daunicht

AU

Dusky Fulvetta
de:Rotkopfalcippe
fr: Alcippe de Gould
es:Fulveta de Gould
ja: チメドリ
cn:褐顶雀鹛
Schoeniparus brunneus

♂ adult

Drawing J.G.Keulemans

PD

♂ adult

PD **Rusty-capped Fulvetta**
de:Olivflanken-Alcippe
fr: Alcippe à calotte rouille
es:Fulveta Coronirrufa
ja:マミジロチメドリ
cn:褐胁雀鹛
Schoeniparus dubius

adult

S2.0 **Puff-throated Babbler**
de:Streifenbrusttimalie
fr: Akalat à poitrine tachetée
es:Charlatán Moteado
ja:ムナフジチメドリ
cn:棕头幽鹛
Pellorneum ruficeps

adult

PD **Spot-throated Babbler**
de:Weißbauch-Erdtimalie
fr: Akalat à gorge tachetée
es:Charlatán Castaño Descolorido
ja:チャイロジチメドリ
cn:白腹幽鹛
Pellorneum albiventre

adult

PD **Buff-breasted Babbler**
de:Rotbrust-Maustimalie
fr: Akalat de Tickell
es:Charlatán del Bosque de la Espesura
ja:チャイロムジチメドリ
cn:棕胸幽鹛
Pellorneum tickelli

Eyebrowed Wren-Babbler

de:Brustfleckentimalie
fr: Petite Turdinule
es:Charlatán-Troglodita Cejudo
ja:コサザイチメドリ
cn:纹胸鹩鹛

Napothera epilepidota

adult

Short-tailed Scimitar Babbler

de:Kurzschwanzsäbler
fr: Pomatorhin à queue courte
es:Charlatán-Cimitarra de Cola Corta
ja:アンナンハシナガチメドリ
cn:短尾鹛

Napothera danjoui

Near threatened.

adult

White-throated Wren-Babbler

de:Vietnamzwergsäbler
fr: Turdinule de Pasquier
es:Ratina Goliblanca
ja:ベトナムサザイチメドリ
cn:白喉鹩鹛

Napothera pasquieri

Endemic.
Endangered.

adult

Abbott's Babbler

de:Rotschwanz-Maustimalie
fr: Akalat d'Abbott
es:Charlatán del Bosque de Abbott
ja:ハシブトムジチメドリ
cn:阿氏雅鹛

Turdinus abbotti

adult

adult

Photo Francesco Veronesi

S2.0

Limestone Wren-Babbler
de: Kalksteintimalie
fr: Turdinule des rochers
es: Charlatán-Troglodita Calizo
ja: クロサザイチメドリ
cn: 灰岩鷦鶥
Turdinus crispifrons

♂ adult

Drawing H.Groenvold

PD

Streaked Wren-Babbler
de: Stutzschwanztimalie
fr: Turdinule à queue courte
es: Ratina Colicorta
ja: ノドフサザイチメドリ
cn: 短尾鷦鶥
Turdinus brevicaudatus

adult

Drawing W.J.Daunicht

AU

Chinese Grassbird
de: Chinagrasdrossling
fr: Graminicole de Chine
es: Yerbera china
ja: チュウゴクコシアカセッカ
cn: 大草莺
Graminicola striatus
Vulnerable.

Laughingthrushes and allies - *Leiothrichidae*

The family of Laughingthrushes is found in Africa and South Asia. Most of the species live in the tropics. They rarely migrate and are rather poor fliers. With almost 150 species, the family is relatively large and very diverse. It was only recently separated in the systematics from the more comprehensive family of Babblers.

Brown-cheeked Fulvetta
　de:Graukopfalcippe
　fr: Alcippe à joues brunes
　es:Fulveta de Mejillas Castañas
　ja:ハイガシラチメドリ
　cn:褐脸雀鹛
Alcippe poioicephala

adult

David's Fulvetta
　de:Davidalcippe
　fr: Alcippe de David
　es:Fulveta de David
　ja:アヴィドチメドリ
　cn:灰眶雀鹛
Alcippe davidi

adult

Mountain Fulvetta
　de:Malaienalcippe
　fr: Alcippe bridé
　es:Fulveta Montañés
　ja:マユグロチメドリ
　cn:山雀鹛
Alcippe peracensis

adult

adult

AU **Black-browed Fulvetta**
de:Weißbauchalcippe
fr: Fulvetta de Grote
es: Fulveta Cejinegra
ja:マユグロチメドリ
cn:黑眉雀鹛
Alcippe grotei

♂ adult

PD **Cutia**
de:Cutia
fr: Cutie du Népal
es: Cutia
ja:セアカチメドリ
cn:斑胁姬鹛
Cutia nipalensis

♂ adult

PD **Vietnamese Cutia**
de:Wellenbauchcutia
fr: Cutie de Le Gallen
es: Cutia Vietnamita
ja:ベトナムセアカチメドリ
cn:越南姬鹛
Cutia legalleni
Endemic.
Near threatened.

adult

PD **Masked Laughingthrush**
de:Maskenhäherling
fr: Garrulaxe masqué
es: Tordo Jocoso de Anteojos
ja:カオグロガビチョウ
cn:黑脸噪鹛
Garrulax perspicillatus

White-crested Laughingthrush
  de:Weißhaubenhäherling
  fr: Garrulaxe à huppe blanche
  es: Tordo Jocoso Gárrulado
  ja: ハクオウチョウ
  cn: 白冠噪鹛
Garrulax leucolophus

adult

AU

Photo W.J.Daunicht

Lesser Necklaced Laughingthrush
  de: Lätzchenhäherling
  fr: Garrulaxe à collier
  es: Tordo Jocoso Chico
  ja: ヒメクビワガビチョウ
  cn: 小黑领噪鹛
Garrulax monileger

adult

AU

Photo W.J.Daunicht

Black-hooded Laughingthrush
  de: Kapuzenhäherling
  fr: Garrulaxe de Millet
  es: Tordo Jocoso de Capucha Negra
  ja: クロズキンガビチョウ
  cn: 黑冠噪鹛
Garrulax milleti
Endemic.
Near threatened.

adult

PD

Drawing H.Groenvold

Grey Laughingthrush
  de: Maeshäherling
  fr: Garrulaxe de Maës
  es: Tordo Jocoso de Maes
  ja: ハイイロガビチョウ
  cn: 褐胸噪鹛
Garrulax maesi

adult

PD

Drawing Juillerat

adult

AU Rufous-cheeked Laughingthrush
de:Rotwangenhäherling
fr: Garrulaxe de Hainan
es:Charlatán Carirrufo
ja:ホオアカガビチョウ
cn:栗頰噪鶥
Garrulax castanotis

Drawing W.J.Daunicht

adult

S2.0 Spot-breasted Laughingthrush
de:Fleckenhäherling
fr: Garrulaxe à poitrine tachetée
es:Tordo Jocoso de Pecho Moteado
ja:ムナボシガビチョウ
cn:斑胸噪鶥
Garrulax merulinus

Photo Francesco Veronesi

adult

PD Orange-breasted Laughingthrush
de:Orangebrusthäherling
fr: Garrulaxe du Lanbian
es:Charlatán Pechinaranja
ja:ベトナムガビチョウ
cn:橙胸噪鶥
Garrulax annamensis
Endemic.

Drawing H.Groenvold

adult

S2.0 Hwamei
de:Augenbrauenhäherling
fr: Garrulaxe hoamy
es:Tordo Jocoso Cantor
ja:ガビチョウ
cn:画眉
Garrulax canorus

Photo Charles Lam

Moustached Laughingthrush
  de:Grauhäherling
  fr: Garrulaxe cendré
  es: Charlatán Ceniciento
  ja: ヒゲガビチョウ
  cn:灰翅噪鹛
Ianthocincla cineracea

adult

Photo Simon Matthews

Rufous-chinned Laughingthrush
  de:Rostkinnhäherling
  fr: Garrulaxe à gorge rousse
  es: Tordo Jocoso de Barbilla Rufa
  ja: キアゴガビチョウ
  cn:棕额噪鹛
Ianthocincla rufogularis

adult

Drawing H.Groenvold

Chestnut-eared Laughingthrush
  de:Braunohrhäherling
  fr: Garrulax à oreilles marron
  es: Tordo Jocoso de Orejas Castañas
  ja: チャミミガビチョウ
  cn:棕耳噪鹛
Ianthocincla konkakinhensis
Endemic.
Vulnerable.

adult

Drawing Charles Eames

Greater Necklaced Laughingthrush
  de:Brustbandhäherling
  fr: Garrulaxe à plastron
  es: Tordo Jocoso Pectoral
  ja: クビワガビチョウ
  cn:黑领噪鹛
Ianthocincla pectoralis

adult

Drawing J.Gould&W.M.Hart

adult

AU White-throated Laughingthrush
de:Weißkehlhäherling
fr: Garrulaxe à gorge blanche
es:Tordo Jocoso de Garganta Blanca
ja: ノドジロガビチョウ
cn:白喉噪鹛
Ianthocincla albogularis

Photo W.J.Daunicht

adult

AU Black-throated Laughingthrush
de:Weißohrhäherling
fr: Garrulaxe à joues blanches
es:Tordo Jocoso de Garganta Negra
ja: タイカンチョウ
cn:黑喉噪鹛
Ianthocincla chinensis

Photo W.J.Daunicht

adult

AU White-cheeked Laughingthrush
de:Schwarzohrhäherling
fr: Garrulaxe de Vassal
es:Tordo Jocoso de Mejillas Blancas
ja: ホオジロガビチョウ
cn:白脸噪鹛
Ianthocincla vassali

Drawing W.J.Daunicht

♂♀ adult

PD Rufous-vented Laughingthrush
de:Rotsteißhäherling
fr: Garrulaxe à queue rousse
es:Tordo Jocoso de Subcaudal Rufo
ja: ホオグロガビチョウ
cn:栗臀噪鹛
Ianthocincla gularis

Drawing J.Gould&H.C.Richter

White-browed Laughingthrush
de:Weißwangenhäherling
fr: Garrulaxe à sourcils blancs
es: Tordo Jocoso de Cejas Blancas
ja: カオジロガビチョウ
cn:白颊噪鹛
Ianthocincla sannio

adult

Scaly Laughingthrush
de:Goldschwingenhäherling
fr: Garrulaxe modeste
es: Tordo Jocoso Descolorido
ja: ウロコガビチョウ
cn:纯色噪鹛
Trochalopteron subunicolor

adult

Blue-winged Laughingthrush
de:Blauflügelhäherling
fr: Garrulaxe écaillé
es: Tordo Jocoso de Alas Azules
ja: アオバネガビチョウ
cn:鳞斑噪鹛
Trochalopteron squamatum

adult

Black-faced Laughingthrush
de:Schwarzscheitelhäherling
fr: Garrulaxe à face noire
es: Tordo Jocoso de Cara Negra
ja: キンバネガビチョウ
cn:黑顶噪鹛
Trochalopteron affine

adult

adult

S2.0

Silver-eared Laughingthrush
de:Silberohrhäherling
fr: Garrulax de Blyth
es:Charlatán Orejiplateado
ja: ハイミミガビチョウ
cn:银耳噪鹛
Trochalopteron melanostigma

Photo Francesco Veronesi

adult

S3.0

Golden-winged Laughingthrush
de:Goldflügelhäherling
fr: Garrulaxe du Ngoc Linh
es:Charlatán Alidorado
ja: キンバネガビチョウ
cn:金翅噪鹛
Trochalopteron ngoclinhense
Endemic.
Vulnerable.

Drawing Kamol Komolphalin

adult

PD

Collared Laughingthrush
de:Halsbandhäherling
fr: Garrulaxe de Yersin
es:Tordo Jocoso de Yersin
ja: ギンミミガビチョウ
cn:纹枕噪鹛
Trochalopteron yersini
Endemic.
Endangered.

Drawing H.Groenvold

adult

AU

Red-winged Laughingthrush
de:Prachthäherling
fr: Garrulaxe élégant
es:Tordo Jocoso de Alas Carmín
ja: アカバネガビチョウ
cn:红翅噪鹛
Trochalopteron formosum

Photo W.J.Daunicht

Red-tailed Laughingthrush
de:Rotschwanzhäherling
fr: Garrulaxe à queue rouge
es: Tordo Jocoso de Cola Roja
ja: アカオガビチョウ
cn:红尾噪鹛
Trochalopteron milnei

adult

Black-headed Sibia
de:Schwarzkopftimalie
fr: Sibia de Desgodins
es: Sibia de Desgodins
ja: クロガシラウタイチメドリ
cn:黑耳奇鹛
Heterophasia desgodinsi

adult

Long-tailed Sibia
de:Schweiftimalie
fr: Sibia à longue queue
es: Sibia de Cola Larga
ja: オナガウタイチメドリ
cn:长尾奇鹛
Heterophasia picaoides

adult

Silver-eared Leiothrix
de:Silberohr-Sonnenvogel
fr: Léiothrix à joues argent
es: Leiothrix de Mejillas Argénteas
ja: ゴシキソウシチョウ
cn:银耳相思鸟
Leiothrix argentauris

♂ adult

adult

Red-billed Leiothrix
AU
de:Sonnenvogel
fr: Léiothrix jaune
es: Leiothrix de Pico Rojo
ja: ソウシチョウ
cn:红嘴相思鸟
Leiothrix lutea

Photo W.J.Daunicht

adult

Red-tailed Minla
PD
de:Rotschwanzsiva
fr: Minla à queue rousse
es: Minla de Cola Roja
ja: アカオコバシチメドリ
cn:火尾希鹛
Minla ignotincta

Drawing H.Groenvold

adult

Rufous-backed Sibia
PD
de:Rotrückentimalie
fr: Sibia à dos marron
es: Minla de Lomo Castaño
ja: セアカウタイチメドリ
cn:栗背奇鹛
Minla annectens

Drawing W.M.Hart

adult

Grey-crowned Crocias
S4.0
de:Grauscheitel-Würgertimalie
fr: Sibia du Langbian
es: Sibia del Monte Langbian
ja: ワキフチメドリ
cn:灰冠南洋鹛
Crocias langbianis
Endemic.
Endangered.

Drawing Pham Quang

Scarlet-faced Liocichla
 de: Burma-Karminflügelhäherling
 fr: Garrulaxe de Rippon
 es: Charlatán de Rippon
 ja: ヒガオヤブドリ
 cn: 红翅薮鹛
Liocichla ripponi

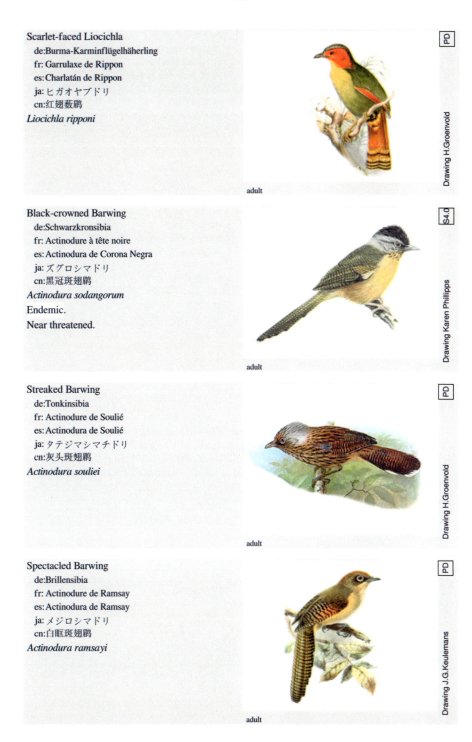

adult

PD · Drawing H.Groenvold

Black-crowned Barwing
 de: Schwarzkronsibia
 fr: Actinodure à tête noire
 es: Actinodura de Corona Negra
 ja: ズグロシマドリ
 cn: 黑冠斑翅鹛
Actinodura sodangorum
Endemic.
Near threatened.

adult

S4.0 · Drawing Karen Phillipps

Streaked Barwing
 de: Tonkinsibia
 fr: Actinodure de Soulié
 es: Actinodura de Soulié
 ja: タテジマシマチドリ
 cn: 灰头斑翅鹛
Actinodura souliei

adult

PD · Drawing H.Groenvold

Spectacled Barwing
 de: Brillensibia
 fr: Actinodure de Ramsay
 es: Actinodura de Ramsay
 ja: メジロシマドリ
 cn: 白眶斑翅鹛
Actinodura ramsayi

adult

PD · Drawing J.G.Keulemans

adult

Drawing H.Goodchild

PD **Blue-winged Minla**
de:Blauflügelsiva
fr: Minla à ailes bleues
es:Minla de Alas Azules
ja:ルリハコバシチメドリ
cn:蓝翅希鹛
Actinodura cyanouroptera

♂♀ adult

Drawing H.Groenvold

PD **Chestnut-tailed Minla**
de:Bändersiva
fr: Minla à gorge striée
es:Minla de Cola Castaña
ja:ノドジマコバシチメドリ
cn:斑喉希鹛
Actinodura strigula

Fairy Bluebirds - *Irenidae*

The only two species of the family of Fairy-bluebirds is found in the tropics of Southeast Asia from India to Borneo and on the Philippines. They are approximately 21.2 cm to 27.5 cm long. Their plumage is bright green or blue and the sexes differ. Their habitat are forests and gardens. They live on fruits, berries, nectar, seeds and buds, supplemented by insects. The nests are flat bowl-shaped and usually contain 2 to 4 eggs.

♂ adult

Photo W.J.Daunicht

AU **Asian Fairy-bluebird**
de:Türkisfeenvogel
fr: Irène vierge
es:Ave Flor de Espalda Negra
ja:ルリコノハドリ
cn:和平鸟
Irena puella

www.avitopia.net/bird.en/?vid=5200101

Flycatchers - *Muscicapidae*

The family of Flycatchers occurs in Africa, Europe and Asia. Many species are long-distance migrants. The body length ranges from 9 cm to 20 cm. Flycatchers have relatively long legs and are often strikingly colored. They mainly eat insects, but also plant-based foods.

Grey-streaked Flycatcher
  de:Strichelschnäpper
  fr: Gobemouche à taches grises
  es:Papamoscas de Lineas Grises
  ja:エゾビタキ
  cn:灰纹鶲
Muscicapa griseisticta

adult

Dark-sided Flycatcher
  de:Rußschnäpper
  fr: Gobemouche de Sibérie
  es:Papamoscas Siberiano
  ja:サメビタキ
  cn:乌鶲
Muscicapa sibirica

adult

Ferruginous Flycatcher
  de:Rostschnäpper
  fr: Gobemouche ferrugineux
  es:Papamoscas Ferruginoso
  ja:ミヤマヒタキ
  cn:棕尾褐鶲
Muscicapa ferruginea

adult

adult

Photo W.J.Daunicht

AU

Asian Brown Flycatcher
de:Braunschnäpper
fr: Gobemouche brun
es:Papamoscas Castaño
ja:コサメビタキ
cn:北灰鶲
Muscicapa dauurica

adult

Drawing J.G.Keulemans

PD

Brown-breasted Flycatcher
de:Bambusschnäpper
fr: Gobemouche muttui
es:Papamoscas de Pecho Castaño
ja:チャムネサメビタキ
cn:褐胸鶲
Muscicapa muttui

adult

Drawing W.J.Daunicht

AU

Brown-streaked Flycatcher
de:Williamsonschnäpper
fr: Gobemouche de Williamson
es:Papamoscas de Williamson
ja:ミナミコサメビタキ
cn:褐纹鶲
Muscicapa williamsoni

♂ adult

Photo W.J.Daunicht

AU

Oriental Magpie-Robin
de:Dajaldrossel
fr: Shama dayal
es:Shama Oriental
ja:シキチョウ
cn:鹊鸲
Copsychus saularis

White-rumped Shama
de: Schamadrossel
fr: Shama à croupion blanc
es: Mirlo Shama Hindú
ja: アカハラシキチョウ
cn: 白腰鹊鸲

Copsychus malabaricus

www.avitopia.net/bird.en/?vid=5250907

adult

White-gorgeted Flycatcher
de: Diamantschnäpper
fr: Gobemouche à gorge blanche
es: Papamoscas de Gargantilla Blanca
ja: ノドジロヒタキ
cn: 白喉姬鹟

Anthipes monileger

adult

Rufous-browed Flycatcher
de: Roststirnschnäpper
fr: Gobemouche à face rousse
es: Papamoscas Solitario
ja: アカメヒタキ
cn: 棕眉姬鹟

Anthipes solitaris

adult

White-tailed Flycatcher
de: Weißschwanz-Blauschnäpper
fr: Gobemouche à queue blanche
es: Niltava de Cola Blanca
ja: オジロアオヒタキ
cn: 白尾蓝仙鹟

Cyornis concretus

♂ adult

adult

Photo Rushenb

A2.0

Hainan Blue Flycatcher
de:Hainanblauschnäpper
fr: Gobemouche de Hainan
es: Niltava de Grant
ja: ハイナンヒメアオヒタキ
cn: 海南蓝仙鹟
Cyornis hainanus

♂ adult

Drawing H.Groenvold

PD

Pale Blue Flycatcher
de:Blaubrustschnäpper
fr: Gobemouche bleuâtre
es: Niltava Pálida
ja: ウスヒメアオヒタキ
cn: 纯蓝仙鹟
Cyornis unicolor

♂ adult

Photo Jason Thompson

A2.0

Chinese Blue Flycatcher
de:Chinablauschnäpper
fr: Gobemouche du Yunnan
es: Niltava Chino
ja: シナヒメアオヒタキ
cn: 中华仙鹟
Cyornis glaucicomans

♂ adult

Drawing Huet

PD

Hill Blue Flycatcher
de:Bergblauschnäpper
fr: Gobemouche des collines
es: Niltava Azul
ja: ミヤマヒメアオヒタキ
cn: 山蓝仙鹟
Cyornis banyumas

Tickell's Blue Flycatcher
de:Tickellblauschnäpper
fr: Gobemouche de Tickell
es:Niltava de Tickell
ja:ノドアカヒメアオヒタキ
cn:梯氏仙鶲
Cyornis tickelliae

♂ adult

Brown-chested Jungle Flycatcher
de:Weißkehl-Dschungelschnäpper
fr: Gobemouche à poitrine brune
es:Papamoscas Selvático de Gargantilla Blanca
ja:ムナオビミツリンヒタキ
cn:白喉林鶲
Cyornis brunneatus
Vulnerable.

adult

Large Niltava
de:Kobaltblauschnäpper
fr: Grand Gobemouche
es:Niltava Grande
ja:オオアオヒタキ
cn:大仙鶲
Niltava grandis

♂ adult

Small Niltava
de:Feenblauschnäpper
fr: Gobemouche de McGrigor
es:Niltava Chica
ja:チビアオヒタキ
cn:小仙鶲
Niltava macgrigoriae

♂ adult

adult

Drawing unknown

Fujian Niltava
de:Davidblauschnäpper
fr: Gobemouche de David
es: Niltava Platanera
ja: フアキェンアオヒタキ
cn:棕腹大仙鶲
Niltava davidi

Rufous-bellied Niltava
de:Rotbauch-Blauschnäpper
fr: Gobemouche sundara
es: Niltava de Vientre Rufo
ja: コチャバラオオルリ
cn:棕腹仙鶲
Niltava sundara

Drawing J.Gould&H.C.Richter

♂ adult

Vivid Niltava
de:Swinhoeblauschnäpper
fr: Gobemouche à ventre roux
es: Niltava Activa
ja: チャバラオオルリ
cn:棕腹蓝仙鶲
Niltava vivida

Drawing J.Wolf

♂ adult

Blue-and-white Flycatcher
de:Blauschnäpper
fr: Gobemouche bleu
es: Papamoscas Blanco y Azul
ja: オオルリ
cn:白腹蓝鶲
Cyanoptila cyanomelana

Photo W.J.Daunicht

♂ adult

Zappey's Flycatcher
de:Türkisblauschnäpper
fr: Gobemouche de Zappey
es:Papamoscas de Zappey
ja:チョウセンオオルリ
cn:琉璃蓝鹟
Cyanoptila cumatilis
Near threatened.

♂ adult

Drawing unknown

Verditer Flycatcher
de:Lazulischnäpper
fr: Gobemouche vert-de-gris
es:Papamoscas Hindú
ja:ロクショウヒタキ
cn:铜蓝鹟
Eumyias thalassinus

adult

Drawing J.&E.Gould

Gould's Shortwing
de:Braunrücken-Kurzflügel
fr: Brachyptère étoilée
es: Alicorto de Gould
ja:シロボシコバネヒタキ
cn:栗背短翅鹟
Brachypteryx stellata

adult

Drawing J.Gould&H.C.Fichter

Lesser Shortwing
de:Zwergkurzflügel
fr: Petite Brachyptère
es: Alicorto Chico
ja:ヒメコバネヒタキ
cn:白喉短翅鹟
Brachypteryx leucophris

adult

Drawing J.G.Keulemans

♂ adult

PD White-browed Shortwing
de:Bergkurzflügel
fr: Brachyptère bleue
es: Alicorto Azul
ja: コバネヒタキ
cn:蓝短翅鸫
Brachypteryx montana

adult

PD Rufous-tailed Robin
de:Schwirrnachtigall
fr: Rossignol siffleur
es: Petirrojo de Swinhoe
ja: シマゴマ
cn:红尾歌鸲
Larvivora sibilans

adult

S3.0 Japanese Robin
de:Rostkehlnachtigall
fr: Rossignol akahigé
es: Petirrojo Japonés
ja: コマドリ
cn:日本歌鸲
Larvivora akahige

♂ adult

S3.0 Siberian Blue Robin
de:Blaunachtigall
fr: Rossignol bleu
es: Petirrojo Siberiano Azul
ja: コルリ
cn:蓝歌鸲
Larvivora cyane

White-bellied Redstart

de:Kurzflügel-Rotschwanz
fr: Bradybate à queue rouge
es:Collirrojo de Vientre Blanco
ja: オリイヒタキ
cn:短翅鸫

Luscinia phaenicuroides

adult

Drawing J.G.Keulemans

PD

Bluethroat

de:Blaukehlchen
fr: Gorgebleue à miroir
es:Pechiazul
ja: オガワコマドリ
cn:蓝喉歌鸲

Luscinia svecica

♂ adult

Photo W.J.Daunicht

AU

Blue Whistling Thrush

de:Purpurpfeifdrossel
fr: Arrenga siffleur
es: Arrenga Común
ja: オオルリチョウ
cn:紫啸鸫

Myophonus caeruleus

adult

Drawing H.Groenvold

PD

Little Forktail

de:Stummelscherenschwanz
fr: Énicure nain
es:Enicurino Chico
ja: シロクロヒタキ
cn:小燕尾

Enicurus scouleri

♂ adult

Drawing J.Gould&H.C.Richter

PD

adult

PD White-crowned Forktail

de: Weißscheitel-Scherenschwanz
fr: Énicure de Leschenault
es: Enicurino de Corona Blanca
ja: エンビシキチョウ
cn: 白额燕尾
Enicurus leschenaulti

♂ adult

PD Spotted Forktail

de: Fleckenscherenschwanz
fr: Énicure tacheté
es: Enicurino Moteado
ja: セボシエンビシキチョウ
cn: 斑背燕尾
Enicurus maculatus

♂ adult

PD Slaty-backed Forktail

de: Graurücken-Scherenschwanz
fr: Énicure ardoisé
es: Enicurino de Lomo Ahumado
ja: セアオエンビシキチョウ
cn: 灰背燕尾
Enicurus schistaceus

♂ adult

PD Siberian Rubythroat

de: Rubinkehlchen
fr: Rossignol calliope
es: Petirrojo Siberiano
ja: ノゴマ
cn: 红喉歌鸲
Calliope calliope

White-tailed Robin
de:Schattenschmätzer
fr: Notodèle à queue blanche
es: Ruiseñor Coliblanco
ja: コンヒタキ
cn:白尾地鸲
Myiomela leucura

adult

Blue-fronted Robin
de:Blauschmätzer
fr: Notodèle à front bleu
es: Ruiseñor Frentiazul
ja: オグロコンヒタキ
cn:蓝额地鸲
Cinclidium frontale

♂ adult

Red-flanked Bluetail
de:Blauschwanz
fr: Rossignol à flancs roux
es: Coliazul de Cejas Blancas
ja: ルリビタキ
cn:红胁蓝尾鸲
Tarsiger cyanurus

♂ adult

Himalayan Bluetail
de:Himalajablauschwanz
fr: Robin de l'Himalaya
es: Ruiseñor del Himalaya
ja: ヒマラヤルリビタキ
cn:蓝眉林鸲
Tarsiger rufilatus

♂ adult

♂ adult

PD White-browed Bush Robin
de:Weißbrauen-Blauschwanz
fr: Rossignol à sourcils blancs
es:Petirrojo de Cejas Blancas
ja: キクチヒタキ
cn:白眉林鴝
Tarsiger indicus

♂ adult

PD Golden Bush Robin
de:Goldschwanz
fr: Rossignol doré
es:Coliazul Dorado
ja: キンイロヒタキ
cn:金色林鴝
Tarsiger chrysaeus

♀ adult

S2.0 Yellow-rumped Flycatcher
de:Goldschnäpper
fr: Gobemouche à croupion jaune
es:Papamoscas de Lomo Amarillo
ja: マミジロキビタキ
cn:白眉姬鶲
Ficedula zanthopygia

♂ adult

AU Chinese Flycatcher
de:Elisenschnäpper
fr: Gobemouche à dos vert
es:Papamoscas de Elisa
ja: チャイニアズヒタキ
cn:绿背姬鶲
Ficedula elisae

Narcissus Flycatcher
de:Narzissenschnäpper
fr: Gobemouche narcisse
es: Papamoscas de Narciso
ja: キビタキ
cn: 黄眉姫鶲
Ficedula narcissina

PD

Drawing unknown

♂ adult

Mugimaki Flycatcher
de: Mugimakischnäpper
fr: Gobemouche mugimaki
es: Papamoscas de Mugimaki
ja: ムギマキ
cn: 鸲姫鶲
Ficedula mugimaki

PD

Drawing Pretre

♂ adult

Slaty-backed Flycatcher
de: Hodgsonschnäpper
fr: Gobemouche de Hodgson
es: Papamoscas de Pechos Rojizo
ja: セアオヒタキ
cn: 锈胸蓝姫鶲
Ficedula sordida

PD

Drawing Huet

adult

Slaty-blue Flycatcher
de: Dreifarbenschnäpper
fr: Gobemouche bleu-ardoise
es: Papamoscas Tricolor
ja: カオグロヒタキ
cn: 灰蓝姫鶲
Ficedula tricolor

PD

Drawing J.G.Keulemans

♂ adult

♂ adult

Photo Lip Kee Yap

S2.0

Snowy-browed Flycatcher
de:Rotbrust-Grundschnäpper
fr: Gobemouche givré
es:Papamoscas de la Espesura
ja: ムネアカヒタキ
cn:棕胸蓝姬鹟
Ficedula hyperythra

♂ adult

Drawing J.Wolf

PD

Pygmy Flycatcher
de:Goldhähnchen-Blauschnäpper
fr: Gobemouche pygmée
es:Niltava Pigmea
ja: コビトアオヒタキ
cn:侏蓝仙鹟
Ficedula hodgsoni

adult

Drawing I.Schubert

PD

Rufous-gorgeted Flycatcher
de:Zimtkehlschnäpper
fr: Gobemouche à bavette orange
es:Papamoscas de Gargantilla Anaranjada
ja: ノドグロヒタキ
cn:橙胸姬鹟
Ficedula strophiata

adult

Drawing Leonard

PD

Sapphire Flycatcher
de:Saphirschnäpper
fr: Gobemouche saphir
es:Papamoscas Safiro
ja: サファイヤヒタキ
cn:玉头姬鹟
Ficedula sapphira

Little Pied Flycatcher
de:Elsterschnäpper
fr: Gobemouche pie
es: Papamoscas Pálido Chico
ja: ハジロマユヒタキ
cn:小斑姬鶲
Ficedula westermanni

♂ adult

Taiga Flycatcher
de:Taigaschnäpper
fr: Gobemouche de la Taïga
es: Papamoscas de la Taiga
ja: オジロビタキ
cn:红喉姬鶲
Ficedula albicilla

♂ adult

Blue-fronted Redstart
de:Himalayarotschwanz
fr: Rougequeue à front bleu
es: Colirrojo de Patas Azules
ja: ルリビタイジョウビタキ
cn:蓝额红尾鸲
Phoenicurus frontalis

♂ adult

Plumbeous Water-Redstart
de:Wasserrotschwanz
fr: Nymphée fuligineuse
es: Colirrojo Fuliginoso
ja: カワビタキ
cn:红尾水鸲
Phoenicurus fuliginosus

adult

Photo Panki sood

S3.0

adult

White-capped Redstart
de:Weißkopf-Rotschwanz
fr: Torrentaire à calotte blanche
es:Colirrojo de Capa Blanca
ja: シロボウシカワビタキ
cn:白顶溪鸲
Phoenicurus leucocephalus

Photo W.J.Daunicht

AU

♂ adult

Daurian Redstart
de:Spiegelrotschwanz
fr: Rougequeue aurore
es:Colirrojo Dáurico
ja: ジョウビタキ
cn:北红尾鸲
Phoenicurus auroreus

Drawing J.Gould&H.C.Richter

PD

♂ adult

Chestnut-bellied Rock Thrush
de:Rötelmerle
fr: Monticole à ventre marron
es:Roquero de Vientre Castaño
ja: カオグロイソヒヨドリ
cn:栗腹矶鸫
Monticola rufiventris

Drawing unknown

PD

♂ adult

White-throated Rock Thrush
de:Amurrötel
fr: Monticole à gorge blanche
es:Roquero de Garganta Blanca
ja: ヒメイソヒヨ
cn:白喉矶鸫
Monticola gularis

Blue Rock Thrush
de:Blaumerle
fr: Monticole merle-bleu
es: Roquero Solitario
ja: イソヒヨドリ
cn:蓝矶鸫
Monticola solitarius

♂ adult

Siberian Stonechat
de:Sibirisches Schwarzkehlchen
fr: Tarier de Sibérie
es: Tarabilla común siberiana
ja: ノビタキ
cn:黑喉石鴫
Saxicola maurus

♂ adult

Pied Bush Chat
de:Mohrenschwarzkehlchen
fr: Tarier pie
es: Tarabilla Pálida
ja: クロノビタキ
cn:白斑黑石(即鸟)
Saxicola caprata

adult

Jerdon's Bush Chat
de:Jerdonschmätzer
fr: Tarier de Jerdon
es: Tarabilla de Jerdon
ja: クロシロノビタキ
cn:黑白林鴫
Saxicola jerdoni

♂ adult

PD Grey Bush Chat
de:Grauschmätzer
fr: Tarier gris
es:Tarabilla Gris
ja:ヤマザキヒタキ
cn:灰林(即鸟)
Saxicola ferreus

Drawing J.G.Keulemans

♂ adult

Thrushes - *Turdidae*

The family of Thrushes is distributed worldwide and is even found on many small islands in the Pacific, only missing in Antarctica and New Zealand. But Blackbirds and Song thrushes have been introduced there and have reproduced so much that they are now among the most common birds. Thrushes mainly feed on insects and other invertebrates, but berries also play a role in winter.

S3.0 Siberian Thrush
de:Schieferdrossel
fr: Grive de Sibérie
es:Zorzal de Siberia
ja:マミジロ
cn:白眉地鸫
Geokichla sibirica

Photo M.Nishimura

♂ adult

AU Orange-headed Thrush
de:Damadrossel
fr: Grive à tête orange
es:Zorzal Dama
ja:オレンジジツグミ
cn:橙头地鸫
Geokichla citrina

Photo W.J.Daunicht

adult

Long-tailed Thrush
  de:Dixondrossel
  fr: Grive de Dixon
  es:Zorzal Coludo
  ja:オナガトラツグミ
  cn:长尾地鸫
Zoothera dixoni

adult

Drawing J.G.Keulemans

PD

Himalayan Thrush
  de:Walderddrossel
  fr: Grive de Salim Ali
  es:Zorzal de Salim Ali
  ja: ヒマラヤトラツグミ
  cn:喜马拉雅地鸫
Zoothera salimalii

adult

Photo Craig Brelsford

A4.0

Sichuan Thrush
  de:Sichuanerddrossel
  fr: Grive du Sichuan
  es:Zorzal dorsiliso de Sichuan
  ja: シセントラツグミ
  cn:四川地鸫
Zoothera griseiceps

adult

Photo John&Jemi Holmes

A4.0

Dark-sided Thrush
  de:Langschnabeldrossel
  fr: Grive à grand bec
  es:Zorzal Picudo Chico
  ja:コオオハシツグミ
  cn:长嘴地鸫
Zoothera marginata

adult

Photo Jon Hornbuckle

S4.0

adult, juvenile

PD Long-billed Thrush
de:Bergdrossel
fr: Grive montagnarde
es:Zorzal Picudo Grande
ja: オオハシツグミ
cn:大长嘴地鸫
Zoothera monticola

adult

S2.0 White's Thrush
de:Whitedrossel
fr: Grive de White
es:Zorzal de White
ja: トラツグミ
cn:怀氏虎鸫
Zoothera aurea

♂ adult

PD Scaly Thrush
de:Erddrossel
fr: Grive dorée
es:Zorzal Dorado
ja: トラツグミ
cn:虎斑地鸫
Zoothera dauma

adult

PD Grey-backed Thrush
de:Gartendrossel
fr: Merle à dos gris
es:Zorzal Dorsigrís
ja: カラアカハラ
cn:灰背鸫
Turdus hortulorum

Black-breasted Thrush
de:Schwarzbrustdrossel
fr: Merle à poitrine noire
es:Zorzal Pechinegro
ja:ムナグロアカハラ
cn:黑胸鸫
Turdus dissimilis

♂ adult

Japanese Thrush
de:Scheckendrossel
fr: Merle du Japon
es:Zorzal Japonés
ja: クロツグミ
cn:乌灰鸫
Turdus cardis

adult

Grey-winged Blackbird
de:Bülbülamsel
fr: Merle à ailes grises
es:Mirlo de Alas Grises
ja:ハイバネツグミ
cn:灰翅鸫
Turdus boulboul

♂ adult

Chinese Blackbird
de:Mandarinamsel
fr: Merle oriental
es:Mirlo Oriental
ja: クロウタドリ
cn:乌鸫
Turdus mandarinus

♂♀ adult

♂♀ adult

Drawing J.Gould&H.C.Richter

PD Chestnut Thrush
   de:Kastaniendrossel
   fr: Merle à tête grise
   es:Mirlo de Cabeza Gris
   ja: クリイロツグミ
   cn:灰头鸫
Turdus rubrocanus

adult

Photo M.Nishimura

S3.0 Eyebrowed Thrush
   de:Weißbrauendrossel
   fr: Merle obscur
   es:Zorzal Rojigrís
   ja: マミチャジナイ
   cn:白眉鸫
Turdus obscurus

♂ adult

Drawing B.Geisler

PD Dusky Thrush
   de:Rostflügeldrossel
   fr: Grive à ailes rousses
   es:Zorzal eunomo
   ja: ツグミ
   cn:斑鸫
Turdus eunomus

♂ adult

Drawing J.Gould&H.C.Richter

PD Purple Cochoa
   de:Purpurschnäpperdrossel
   fr: Cochoa pourpré
   es:Cochoa Purpúrea
   ja: ムラサキミヤマツグミ
   cn:紫宽嘴鸫
Cochoa purpurea

Green Cochoa
  de:Smaragdschnäpperdrossel
  fr: Cochoa vert
  es: Cochoa Verde
  ja: ミドリミヤマツグミ
  cn: 绿宽嘴鸫
Cochoa viridis

♂ adult

Starlings - *Sturnidae*

The family of Starlings was originally only distributed in the Old World, but the common star was introduced in America and is now widespread there. The body length ranges from 18 cm to 43 cm. Many species have iridescent plumage. The tail is usually short, more rarely long. Unlike Thrushes, Starlings do not hop, but run with alternating steps. They fly well and the formation flights of large flocks of Starlings are impressive. Most species breed in tree hollows, but other nesting techniques also occur, including large community nests. Starlings are omnivores, one reason for their assertiveness as colonists.

Golden-crested Myna
  de:Kronenatzel
  fr: Martin couronné
  es: Mainá de Cresta Dorada
  ja: キガシラムクドリ
  cn: 金冠树八哥
Ampeliceps coronatus

www.avitopia.net/bird.en/?kom=5326001

♂ adult

Common Hill Myna
  de:Beo
  fr: Mainate religieux
  es: Mainá del Himalaya
  ja: キュウカンチョウ
  cn: 鹩哥
Gracula religiosa

adult

adult

Photo NatureAtYourBackyard

A2.0

Daurian Starling
de: Mongolenstar
fr: Étourneau de Daourie
es: Estornino Daurio
ja: シベリアムクドリ
cn: 北椋鸟
Agropsar sturninus

adult

Drawing W.J.Swainson

PD

Black-collared Starling
de: Schwarzhalsstar
fr: Étourneau à cou noir
es: Estornino de Collar Negro
ja: クビワムクドリ
cn: 黑领椋鸟
Gracupica nigricollis

adult

Photo W.J.Daunicht

AU

Pied Myna
de: Elsterstar
fr: Étourneau pie
es: Estornino Pálido Asiático
ja: ホオジロムクドリ
cn: 斑椋鸟
Gracupica contra

adult

Photo Olaf Oliviero Riemer

S3.0

White-shouldered Starling
de: Mandarinstar
fr: Étourneau mandarin
es: Estornino Chino
ja: カラムクドリ
cn: 灰背椋鸟
Sturnia sinensis

Chestnut-tailed Starling
de:Graukopfstar
fr: Étourneau à tête grise
es: Estornino de Cabeza Ceniza
ja: インドコムクドリ
cn:灰头椋鸟
Sturnia malabarica

PD

Drawing W.Rutledge

adult

Red-billed Starling
de:Seidenstar
fr: Étourneau soyeux
es: Estornino Sedoso
ja: ギンムクドリ
cn:丝光椋鸟
Spodiopsar sericeus

PD

Drawing W.J.Swainson

♂ adult

White-cheeked Starling
de:Weißwangenstar
fr: Étourneau gris
es: Estornino Gris
ja: ムクドリ
cn:灰椋鸟
Spodiopsar cineraceus

PD

Drawing Pretre

adult

Common Myna
de:Hirtenmaina
fr: Martin triste
es: Mainá Común
ja: カバイロハッカ
cn:家八哥
Acridotheres tristis

AU

Photo W.J.Daunicht

adult

AU

adult

Vinous-breasted Starling
  de: Burmastar
  fr: Étourneau vineux
  es: Estornino de Jerdon
  ja: シロガシラムクドリ
  cn: 红嘴椋鸟
Acridotheres burmannicus

Photo W.J.Daunicht

A3.0

adult

Great Myna
  de: Langschopfmaina
  fr: Grand Martin
  es: Mainá Grande
  ja: オオハッカ
  cn: 林八哥
Acridotheres grandis

Photo JJ Harrison

AU

adult

Crested Myna
  de: Haubenmaina
  fr: Martin huppé
  es: Mainá China
  ja: ハッカチョウ
  cn: 八哥
Acridotheres cristatellus

Photo W.J.Daunicht

Leafbirds - *Chloropseidae*

The family of Leafbirds lives in the tropical Indian subcontinent and Southeast Asia. Their length ranges from 14 cm to 21 cm. By far the dominant color of the plumage is green, but there are gender differences in almost all species. Their habitat are the treetops in forests of various kinds. They mainly feed on insects, but also on fruits and nectar. When caught, they lose a lot of body feathers. The nests are open and cup-shaped, mostly high in the tree and 2 to 3 eggs are laid in them. Apparently they are only incubated by the females.

Blue-winged Leafbird
  de:Blauflügel-Blattvogel
  fr: Verdin à tête jaune
  es: Verdín de Alas Azules
  ja: アオバネコノハドリ
  cn:蓝翅叶鹎
Chloropsis cochinchinensis

♂♀ adult

Drawing J.G.Keulemans

Golden-fronted Leafbird
  de:Goldstirn-Blattvogel
  fr: Verdin à front d'or
  es: Verdín de Frente Dorado
  ja: キビタイコノハドリ
  cn:金额叶鹎
Chloropsis aurifrons

♂ adult

Photo W.J.Daunicht

Orange-bellied Leafbird
  de:Orangebauch-Blattvogel
  fr: Verdin de Hardwicke
  es: Verdín de Pico Anaranjado
  ja: アカハラコノハドリ
  cn:橙腹叶鹎
Chloropsis hardwickii

♂ adult

Photo W.J.Daunicht

Flowerpeckers - *Dicaeidae*

The family of Flowerpeckers occurs in Asia and Australia. The small birds are 8 cm to 15 cm long. Many species have small ranges or are even endemic to small islands. Most eat a mixture of fruits and insects, only the Australian species lives almost exclusively on mistletoe. Most Flowerpeckers build hanging nests from plant matter and cobwebs. Both adult birds take care of the offspring.

adult

Drawing J.G.Keulemans

PD Thick-billed Flowerpecker
de:Dickschnabel-Mistelfresser
fr: Dicée à bec épais
es:Pica Flor de Pico Ancho
ja:ハシブトハナドリ
cn:厚嘴啄花鸟
Dicaeum agile

adult

Drawing H.Groenvold

PD Yellow-vented Flowerpecker
de:Gelbsteiß-Mistelfresser
fr: Dicée cul-d'or
es:Pica Flor de Rabo Amarillo
ja:ムナフハナドリ
cn:黄臀啄花鸟
Dicaeum chrysorrheum

adult

Drawing J.G.Keulemans

PD Yellow-bellied Flowerpecker
de:Gelbbauch-Mistelfresser
fr: Dicée à ventre jaune
es:Pica Flor de Vientre Amarillo
ja:キバラハナドリ
cn:黄腹啄花鸟
Dicaeum melanoxanthum

Plain Flowerpecker
de:Olivmistelfresser
fr: Dicée olivâtre
es: Picaflores Sencillo
ja: ムジハナドリ
cn:*纯色啄花鸟
Dicaeum minullum

adult

Fire-breasted Flowerpecker
de:Feuerbrust-Mistelfresser
fr: Dicée à gorge feu
es: Pica Flor de Lomo Verde
ja: ハナドリ
cn:红胸啄花鸟
Dicaeum ignipectus

♂ adult

Scarlet-backed Flowerpecker
de:Scharlachmistelfresser
fr: Dicée à dos rouge
es: Pica Flor de Lomo Carmín
ja: セアカハナドリ
cn:朱背啄花鸟
Dicaeum cruentatum

♂ adult

Sunbirds - *Nectariniidae*

Sunbirds are among the most beautiful birds on earth. They are often mistaken for hummingbirds, but unlike these they belong to the songbirds and do not have their ability to fly. The plumage shimmers in a wide variety of colors, which moreover - like all iridescent colors - vary with the incidence of light. The body length ranges from 8 to 16 cm; some species have elongated central tail feathers, but all have short round wings. The beak is usually thin and curved and is used to pierce petals and soak up the nectar. Typical Sunbird nests consist of cobwebs and soft plant material and hang from branches.

Drawing J.G.Keulemans

♂ adult

PD

Ruby-cheeked Sunbird
de:Rubinwangen-Nektarvogel
fr: Souimanga à joues rubis
es:Nectarina de Mejillas Rojas
ja:ホオアカコバシタイヨウチョウ
cn:紫颊太阳鸟
Chalcoparia singalensis

Photo HowardB

♂ adult

S3.0

Brown-throated Sunbird
de:Braunkehl-Nektarvogel
fr: Souimanga à gorge brune
es:Nectarina de Garganta Descolorida
ja:チャノドコバシタイヨウチョウ
cn:褐喉食蜜鸟
Anthreptes malacensis

Drawing J.G.Keulemans

♂ adult

PD

Van Hasselt's Sunbird
de:Blauglanz-Nektarvogel
fr: Souimanga de Hasselt
es:Suimanga ventrigranate
ja:アンハッセルトタイヨウチョウ
cn:紫喉蓝肩花蜜鸟
Leptocoma brasiliana

Copper-throated Sunbird
 de:Kupferkehl-Nektarvogel
 fr: Souimanga de Macklot
 es: Nectarina de Macklot
 ja: ノドアカタイヨウチョウ
 cn:铜喉花蜜鸟
Leptocoma calcostetha

♂ adult

Drawing J.G.Keulemans

Purple Sunbird
 de:Purpurnektarvogel
 fr: Souimanga asiatique
 es: Nectarina Asiática
 ja: ムラサキタイヨウチョウ
 cn:紫色花蜜鸟
Cinnyris asiaticus

♂ breeding

Drawing J.G.Keulemans

Olive-backed Sunbird
 de:Grünrücken-Nektarvogel
 fr: Souimanga à dos vert
 es: Nectarina de Lomo Olivo
 ja: キバラタイヨウチョウ
 cn:黄腹花蜜鸟
Cinnyris jugularis

♂ adult

Photo W.J.Daunicht

Black-throated Sunbird
 de:Schwarzkehl-Nektarvogel
 fr: Souimanga sombre
 es: Nectarina de Garganta Negra
 ja: ムナグロタイヨウチョウ
 cn:黑胸太阳鸟
Aethopyga saturata

adult

Drawing J.G.Keulemans

♂ adult

PD **Mrs. Gould's Sunbird**
de:Gouldnektarvogel
fr: Souimanga de Gould
es: Nectarina de la Sra. Gould
ja: ルリオタイヨウチョウ
cn:蓝喉太阳鸟
Aethopyga gouldiae

♂ adult

PD **Green-tailed Sunbird**
de:Grünschwanz-Nektarvogel
fr: Souimanga à queue verte
es: Nectarina de Cola Verde
ja: ミドリオタイヨウチョウ
cn:绿喉太阳鸟
Aethopyga nipalensis

♂ adult

S2.0 **Crimson Sunbird**
de:Karmesinnektarvogel
fr: Souimanga siparaja
es: Suimanga Siparaja
ja: キゴシタイヨウチョウ
cn:黄腰太阳鸟
Aethopyga siparaja

♂ adult

PD **Fork-tailed Sunbird**
de:Hainannektarvogel
fr: Souimanga de Christine
es: Nectarina Tijereta
ja: エンビタイヨウチョウ
cn:叉尾太阳鸟
Aethopyga christinae

Little Spiderhunter

    de:Weißkehl-Spinnenjäger

    fr: Petit Arachnothère

    es: Arañera Pequeña

    ja: ハシナガクモカリドリ

    cn:长嘴捕蛛鸟

Arachnothera longirostra

adult

Purple-naped Sunbird

    de:Streifennektarvogel

    fr: Souimanga strié

    es: Nectarina de Nuca Azul

    ja: ムナフタイヨウチョウ

    cn:蓝枕花蜜鸟

Arachnothera hypogrammicum

♂ adult

Streaked Spiderhunter

    de:Strichelspinnenjäger

    fr: Grand Arachnothère

    es: Arañera Rayada

    ja: タテジマクモカリドリ

    cn:纹背捕蛛鸟

Arachnothera magna

adult

Wagtails and Pipits - *Motacillidae*

The family of Wagtails is found worldwide except in the coldest areas, many species are migratory birds. They are slender birds with a body length of 13 cm to 22 cm. All species are ground birds, but they can also fly well. First and foremost, they are insectivores.

adult

Drawing J.Gould&H.C.Richter

PD Forest Wagtail
   de:Baumstelze
   fr: Bergeronnette de forêt
   es:Lavandera Forestal
   ja: イワミセキレイ
   cn:山鹡鸰
   Dendronanthus indicus

adult

Drawing L.A.Fuertes

PD Eastern Yellow Wagtail
   de:Ostschafstelze
   fr: Bergeronnette de Béringie
   es:Lavandera Siberiana
   ja: ヒガシセキレイ
   cn:黄鹡鸰
   Motacilla tschutschensis

adult

Photo Alastair Rae

S2.0 Citrine Wagtail
   de:Zitronenstelze
   fr: Bergeronnette citrine
   es:Lavandera Cetrina
   ja: キガシラセキレイ
   cn:黄头鹡鸰
   Motacilla citreola

Grey Wagtail
de:Gebirgsstelze
fr: Bergeronnette des ruisseaux
es: Lavandera Cascadeña
ja: キセキレイ
cn:灰鹡鸰
Motacilla cinerea

AU
Photo W.J.Daunicht
♂ adult

White Wagtail
de:Bachstelze
fr: Bergeronnette grise
es: Lavandera Blanca
ja: タイリクハクセキレイ
cn:白鹡鸰
Motacilla alba

www.avitopia.net/bird.en/?kom=5475308
www.avitopia.net/bird.en/?vid=5475308

AU
Photo W.J.Daunicht
♂ adult

Mekong Wagtail
de:Mekongstelze
fr: Bergeronnette du Mékong
es: Lavandera del Mekong
ja: メコンセキレイ
cn:湄公鹡鸰
Motacilla samveasnae
Near threatened.

S3.0
Photo Pete Davidson
♂ adult

Richard's Pipit
de:Spornpieper
fr: Pipit de Richard
es: Bisbita de Richard
ja: マミジロタヒバリ
cn:田鹨
Anthus richardi

AU
Photo W.J.Daunicht
adult

adult

Paddyfield Pipit
de:Orientspornpieper
fr: Pipit rousset
es:Bisbita Oriental
ja: ヒメマミジロタヒバリ
cn:东方田鹨
Anthus rufulus

adult

Rosy Pipit
de:Rosenpieper
fr: Pipit rosé
es:Bisbita Rosado
ja: チョウセンタヒバリ
cn:粉红胸鹨
Anthus roseatus

adult

Olive-backed Pipit
de:Waldpieper
fr: Pipit à dos olive
es:Bisbita de Hodgson
ja: ビンズイ
cn:树鹨
Anthus hodgsoni

adult

Red-throated Pipit
de:Rotkehlpieper
fr: Pipit à gorge rousse
es:Bisbita Gorgirrojo
ja: ムネアカタヒバリ
cn:红喉鹨
Anthus cervinus

Water Pipit
de:Bergpieper
fr: Pipit spioncelle
es:Bisbita Alpino
ja: タヒバリ
cn:水鹨
Anthus spinoletta

adult

Buff-bellied Pipit
de:Pazifischer Wasserpieper
fr: Pipit d'Amérique
es:Bisbita Norteamericano
ja: アメリカタヒバリ
cn:黄腹鹨
Anthus rubescens

adult

Spotted Elachura - *Elachuridae*

The only species of the family of Spotted Elachuras occurs in Southeast Asia from Nepal to Vietnam and southern China. For a long time it was placed with the Timalia, but after biomolecular studies it was given a family of its own. It is about 10 cm tall. Its habitat are temperate and subtropical forests, in which they stay in the undergrowth. The dome-shaped nest made of plant material is hidden on the ground, the clutch consists of three to four eggs.

Spotted Wren-Babbler
de:Fleckenbrust-Zaunkönigstimalie
fr: Timalie tachetée
es:Ratina Moteada
ja: シロボシサザイチメドリ
cn:丽星鹩鹛
Elachura formosa

adult

Old World Buntings - *Emberizidae*

The family od Old World Buntings is restricted zo the Old World, i.e. to Eurasia and Africa. They are stubby little birds with conical beaks. They feed on seeds. This family was only recently separated from the earlier, much larger-sized family of Buntings in the system of birds on the basis of DNA studies.

Photo Dr Raju Kasambe

adult

Crested Bunting
de: Haubenammer
fr: Bruant huppé
es: Pinzón Copetón
ja: レンジャクノジコ
cn: 风头鹀
Melophus lathami

Photo Alnus

adult

Tristram's Bunting
de: Tristramammer
fr: Bruant de Tristam
es: Escribano de Tristam
ja: シロハラホオジロ
cn: 白眉鹀
Emberiza tristrami

Drawing J.Gould&H.C.Richter

♂ adult

Chestnut-eared Bunting
de: Bandammer
fr: Bruant à oreillons
es: Escribano de Capucha Gris
ja: ホオアカ
cn: 栗耳鹀
Emberiza fucata

Little Bunting
de:Zwergammer
fr: Bruant nain
es:Escribano Pigmeo
ja: コホオアカ
cn:小鵐
Emberiza pusilla

♂ adult

Drawing J.G.Keulemans

Yellow-throated Bunting
de:Gelbkehlammer
fr: Bruant élégant
es:Escribano Elegante
ja: ミヤマホオジロ
cn:黄喉鵐
Emberiza elegans

♂ adult

Drawing J.Gould&W.M.Hart

Yellow-breasted Bunting
de:Weidenammer
fr: Bruant auréole
es:Semillerito de Pecho Amarillo
ja: シマアオジ
cn:黄胸鵐
Emberiza aureola
Endangered.

♂ breeding

Drawing J.G.Keulemans

Chestnut Bunting
de:Rötelammer
fr: Bruant roux
es:Semillerito Castaño
ja: シマノジコ
cn:栗鵐
Emberiza rutila

adult

Drawing unknown

adult

S3.0

Black-faced Bunting
  de:Maskenammer
  fr: Bruant masqué
  es:Escribano de Cara Negra
  ja:アオジ
  cn:灰头鹀
Emberiza spodocephala

Photo M.Nishimura

Finches - *Fringillidae*

The family of Finches is widespread worldwide except for Australia and some oceanic islands. The body length is between 11 cm and 22 cm. They eat seeds and buds, insects almost only during the breeding season. The nest is built by the female from twigs, grass, moss and lichen in the form of a padded bowl.

♂

A2.0

Brambling
  de:Bergfink
  fr: Pinson du Nord
  es:Pinzón Real
  ja:アトリ
  cn:燕雀
Fringilla montifringilla

www.avitopia.net/bird.en/?vid=6125103

Photo mmlolek

♂ adult

PD

Spot-winged Grosbeak
  de:Fleckenkernbeißer
  fr: Gros-bec à ailes tachetées
  es:Pepitero de Alas Moteadas
  ja:キバラクロシメ
  cn:黑腰拟蜡嘴雀
Mycerobas melanozanthos

Drawing J.Gould&H.C.Richter

Yellow-billed Grosbeak
  de:Weißhand-Kernbeißer
  fr: Gros-bec migrateur
  es:Pepitero de Cola Negra
  ja: コイカル
  cn:黑尾蜡嘴雀
Eophona migratoria

adult

Japanese Grosbeak
  de:Maskenkernbeißer
  fr: Gros-bec masqué
  es: Pepitero Enmascarado
  ja: イカル
  cn:黑头蜡嘴雀
Eophona personata

adult

Common Rosefinch
  de:Karmingimpel
  fr: Roselin cramoisi
  es: Camachuelo Carminoso
  ja: アカマシコ
  cn:普通朱雀
Carpodacus erythrinus

♂ adult

Scarlet Finch
  de:Scharlachgimpel
  fr: Cipaye écarlate
  es: Camachuelo Escarlata
  ja: シュイロマシコ
  cn:血雀
Carpodacus sipahi

♂ adult

♂ adult

PD | **Brown Bullfinch**
de:Schuppenkopfgimpel
fr: Bouvreuil brun
es:Camachuelo Castaño
ja: チャイロウソ
cn:褐灰雀
Pyrrhula nipalensis

Drawing H.Groenvold

♂ adult

S4.0 | **Dark-breasted Rosefinch**
de:Dünnschnabelgimpel
fr: Roselin sombre
es:Carpodaco Oscuro
ja: クリムネマシコ
cn:暗胸朱雀
Procarduelis nipalensis

Photo Dibyendu Ash

♂ juvenile

PD | **Grey-capped Greenfinch**
de:Chinagrünling
fr: Verdier de Chine
es: Pardillo Oriental
ja: カワラヒワ
cn:金翅雀
Chloris sinica

Drawing A.Goering

♂ adult

AU | **Vietnamese Greenfinch**
de:Vietnamzeisig
fr: Verdier du Vietnam
es: Verderón Vietnamita
ja: キバラカワラヒワ
cn:越南金翅雀
Chloris monguilloti
Endemic.

Drawing W.J.Daunicht

Black-headed Greenfinch
de: Schwarzkopfgrünling
fr: Verdier d'Oustalet
es: Verderón de Yunnan
ja: ズグロカワラヒワ
cn: 黑头金翅雀
Chloris ambigua

♂ adult

Red Crossbill
de: Fichtenkreuzschnabel
fr: Bec-croisé des sapins
es: Piquitureto Común
ja: イスカ
cn: 红交嘴雀
Loxia curvirostra

♂ adult

Eurasian Siskin
de: Erlenzeisig
fr: Tarin des aulnes
es: Lúgano
ja: マヒワ
cn: 黄雀
Spinus spinus

www.avitopia.net/bird.en/?vid=6129902

♂ adult

Sparrows - *Passeridae*

The sparrow family is native to Europe, Asia and Africa. However, one species managed to conquer the entire globe. The small birds are only 10 cm to 18 cm long. The conical beak indicates that they are grain eaters.

♂ adult

AU

House Sparrow
de:Haussperling
fr: Moineau domestique
es:Gorrión Doméstico
ja: イエスズメ
cn:家麻雀
Passer domesticus

www.avitopia.net/bird.en/?vid=6150202
www.avitopia.net/bird.en/?aud=6150202

Photo W.J.Daunicht

♂ adult

PD

Russet Sparrow
de:Rötelsperling
fr: Moineau rutilant
es:Gorrión Acanelado
ja:ニュウナイスズメ
cn:山麻雀
Passer rutilans

Drawing J.G.Keulemans

adult

PD

Plain-backed Sparrow
de:Gelbbauchsperling
fr: Moineau flavéole
es:Gorrión de Pegu
ja:セアカスズメ
cn:黄腹麻雀
Passer flaveolus

Drawing H.Groenvold

Eurasian Tree Sparrow
  de:Feldsperling
  fr: Moineau friquet
  es: Gorrión Molinero
  ja: コガネスズメ
  cn:麻雀
Passer montanus

🔊 www.avitopia.net/bird.en/?kom=6150224

♂ adult

Weavers - *Ploceidae*

The family of Weavers is widespread in Africa, a few species are found in Asia. The body sizes start with 10 cm and reach 70 cm in some species only for the males and only in breeding plumage. Weavers feed on seeds. They are usually gregarious birds and usually breed in colonies. The typical weaver's nest is a closed sphere that hangs from the end of a twig.

Streaked Weaver
  de:Manyarweber
  fr: Tisserin manyar
  es: Tejedor Estriado
  ja: コウヨウジャク
  cn:纹胸织雀
Ploceus manyar

♂ adult

Baya Weaver
  de:Bayaweber
  fr: Tisserin baya
  es: Tejedor de Baya
  ja: キムネコウヨウジャク
  cn:黄胸织雀
Ploceus philippinus

♂ adult

Photo Thet Zaw Naing

S2.0

Asian Golden Weaver
  de:Kernbeißerweber
  fr: Tisserin doré
  es:Tejedor Asiático
  ja:キンイロコウヨウジャク
  cn:亚洲金织雀
Ploceus hypoxanthus
Near threatened.

♂ adult

Waxbills - *Estrildidae*

The family of Waxbills is found in Africa, South Asia, and Australia. They are small birds with a body length of 9 cm to 14 cm. The beak is short and strong. Most of the species are grain eaters. As a rule, they are sociable birds. The nests are messy structures that are built by both parents. The chicks' throats are often very contrasting in color. Some species are ready for breeding after just a few months.

Drawing F.W.Frohawk

PD

Red Avadavat
  de:Tigerastrild
  fr: Bengali rouge
  es:Bengalí Rojo
  ja:ベニスズメ
  cn:红梅花雀
Amandava amandava

♂ adult

Drawing H.Goodchild

PD

Pin-tailed Parrot-Finch
  de:Lauchgrüne Papageiamadine
  fr: Diamant quadricolore
  es:Pinzón Loro de Cola Aguda
  ja:セイコウチョウ
  cn:长尾鹦雀
Erythrura prasina

adult

White-rumped Munia
de:Spitzschwanz-Bronzemännchen
fr: Capucin domino
es:Capuchino de Lomo Blanco
ja: コシジロキンパラ
cn:白腰文鸟
Lonchura striata

♂ adult

Scaly-breasted Munia
de:Muskatamadine
fr: Capucin damier
es:Capuchino Nutmeg
ja: シマキンパラ
cn:斑文鸟
Lonchura punctulata

adult

White-bellied Munia
de:Weißbauch-Bronzemännchen
fr: Capucin à ventre blanc
es:Capuchino de Cabeza Blanca
ja: シロハラキンパラ
cn:白胸文鸟
Lonchura leucogastra

adult

Chestnut Munia
de:Schwarzkopfnonne
fr: Capucin à tête noire
es:Capuchino Castaño
ja: ミナミギンパラ
cn:栗腹文鸟
Lonchura atricapilla

adult

adult

AU

White-headed Munia
de: Weißkopfnonne
fr: Capucin à tête blanche
es: Capuchino de Cabeza Pálida
ja: ヘキチョウ
cn: 白头文鸟
Lonchura maja

Photo W.J.Daunicht

adult

AU

Java Sparrow
de: Javareisfink
fr: Padda de Java
es: Gorrión Javanés
ja: ブンチョウ
cn: 禾雀
Lonchura oryzivora
Introduced.
Vulnerable.

Photo W.J.Daunicht

www.avitopia.net/bird.en/?vid=6203231

Indices of Names

Index of English Names

Index of German Names

Index of French Names

283

Index of Spanish Names

Index of Japanese Names

Index of Chinese Names

Index of Scientific Names

Additional Copyright Terms

Made in United States
Cleveland, OH
30 May 2025

17357382R10190